Letters To Sydney

Hope, Faith, & Cancer

By

Heather Jose

First published by AuthorHouse 05/14/04

ISBN: 1-4184-5652-7 (e-book)
ISBN: 1-4184-4664-5 (Paperback)
ISBN: 1-4184-4665-3 (Dust Jacket)

Printed in the United States of America
Bloomington, IN

This book is printed on acid free paper.

Table Of Contents

To the God of miracles,

who sent His Son to die

so that I could live.

And to all of you who joined

in my fight against

Breast Cancer.

Thank you.

Life is not tried, it is merely survived

If you're standing outside the fire.

Garth Brooks

From Standing Outside the Fire

1. Meredith

Sydney Bs,

I am going to rock your world. Me, the one who is suppose to protect you from all the evils of the universe. I'm sure that you can't understand this at 14 months old, but I'm afraid you're going to feel the effects. You see, Mommy has this terrible thing called cancer, and it's threatening our time together. I love you Chunks, and I thought I'd better write it all down. I remember the first time I saw your tiny toes. I couldn't believe how perfectly formed they were, and yet they were so small. Now you are a precious gift toddling around my house. You have this wild blonde hair (where did you get blonde?) that sticks up no matter what. I love it. It completely suits you. I don't know how to prepare you for what is to come other than to promise that I'll take good care of you. People keep telling me that you won't even remember this. I have to say that scares me more than anything right now.

Yours,

Mommy

What is a crisis really? Losing your keys when you're late? Having feelings for someone and not having them returned? These and many other things appear at times to be difficult, but I would never call them a crisis anymore.

It started out as a lighthearted doctor's visit. My husband Larry, my 14-month-old daughter Sydney and I had all gone to my checkup so that we could chat with Meredith. She had gone to medical school with my older brother Troy, and he referred me to her when I called to tell him that I was pregnant. We had all gone through the pregnancy and delivery together and now hadn't seen her since my six-week post delivery checkup. I'll never forget her in the birthing room saying, "It's a girl! Sydney, right?" as soon as she was born.

I was still in a daze, and Meredith having known the names we had chosen for a girl or a boy had already named my baby.

So there we are in the exam room, marveling over Sydney's growth, commenting on Meredith's own pregnancy. I tell her that I came for my yearly check up but that I also had this nagging pain in my sternum that seemed to come and go quite often. As soon as my top half is exposed the questions about my left breast begin. Meredith asks if the nipple has always been retracted. I answer no and redirect her to the pain in my chest.

"It feels muscular," I say. "Do you think it's

from carrying all of my bags all the time?"

I was working as an occupational therapist for a school system. Part of my everyday routine was carrying toy-laden bags in and out of elementary schools. Everyone could always tell a therapist, the one carrying all the bags. They often weighed fifty pounds or more.

I went on to explain that the pain would go away with Tylenol, but that I wanted to know why it was hurting. On a scale of 1 to 10, I'd rank the pain a 4, nothing serious, just bothersome. It had been there for a while though, probably since the summer months.

Meredith continued to focus on my breast and after a few more questions asked if I would mind a colleague coming in to take a look. I told her no, that would be fine. After a quick look and a brief consultation with her in the hall Meredith came back in. I was ready for some answers.

"Isn't that normal? All of my friends said that their breasts changed dramatically throughout pregnancy. I didn't know that I should be concerned about it."

"It's probably nothing," Meredith said," but I want to make sure."

"What could it be?" I asked, wanting a straight answer.

"A cyst, a benign tumor, or," with hesitation because she didn't want to tell me, "it could be cancer."

Imagine that; Me with cancer? I don't even know

5

what cancer is.

We proceed to pack up and go home while Meredith sets up appointments to figure this whole thing out. By the time we are home we've convinced ourselves that we can handle it, and then we'll move on.

No one ever has time to be sick. I had, the week before, resigned from my job to take a similar one closer to home. It would mean less driving, and that I could be working in our home school district where my husband was a high school teacher and head football coach. I was excited about the prospect of working with people who lived in my community, to get to know them on a professional level as well as becoming familiar with the elementary school that Sydney would attend in the future. How would my future employer feel about this? I didn't even have a relationship established yet.

Besides the job thing, how could I have cancer? I am not atypical, and 26 year olds don't get breast cancer. I grew up in a small, uneventful town in southern Michigan. I am a middle child, the only sister to my older brother Troy, and younger brother Josh. We lived a normal life, my mom a computer programmer, my dad a biology teacher at the high school that we all attended. I had done well there, graduated and gone on to college to be an occupational therapist. While in college I met my husband at a YMCA camp where I was working in the summer. Six months after graduation from college we married and two years later Sydney was born. My life had always just rolled along, small ups and downs, but in the scheme of things incidental.

There is nothing like a life filled with incidentals. A life where your biggest worry is about positive changes in your life and the world is at your fingertips.

Faith makes things possible;

It does not make them easy.

Annonymous

2. A Normal Day

Sydney Bs,

So many things to talk about with you. I have so many dreams for you. Seeing you grow, hearing you say new words. Watching you become more than just my daughter, becoming my friend. I keep thinking that everything is going to be okay and then the fear sweeps in again. You make me feel better just by being you these days. You need me to help you grow. Doesn't the cancer know that? I'm going to fight with everything I've got hon. I'm going to watch you grow up.

Mommy

The testing began the next day. Meredith had made some phone calls and Larry and I found ourselves waiting for a mammogram, still not really believing any of this. As we dropped Sydney off with our neighbor Beth that morning she told me that it was nothing, that everything would be fine. The mammogram tech told me that I was awfully young to have breast cancer.

I ended my first day of testing in a small exam room having a biopsy done. The procedure is to insert a needle and try to extract liquid. Liquid is good. It means that it is probably a cyst, and certainly not cancer. A resident was doing the test, with his boss looking on. I should have taken my cue from the older doctor when he asked his resident if he would like him to perform the procedure.

"No, no," the resident answered, "I can do it."

The needle was unable to extract any liquid, and so they moved on to the next procedure, where a sample of the cells is taken from various parts of the lump. This is done with a jagged type of needle, with a hollow core. As we are getting started Meredith comes in, more for reassurance than anything else.

The procedure was painful, and prolonged by the inexperience of the resident, who had to do it repeated times as he was unable to get what he needed. By the end of the procedure I was lying on the table sobbing silently with tears rolling down my temples as I waited for them to leave. Meredith, standing at the end of the table, was holding my ankle, saying she was sorry. I felt as though my life as I knew it had been taken away.

As we once again traveled home it felt as though it couldn't be true. I didn't think a perfectly happy young person could just go to the doctor and find out that they have cancer. I didn't know how to handle any of my new thoughts of cancer and since I had yet to have any answers I just went on, struggling to maintain an emotional balance.

I went to work the next day, having regained my composure with the help of my husband. I even told some of the people that I worked with about the biopsy, confident that it would come back benign.

It isn't just on television that people's lives are changed with one phone call. It happens all the time if you think about it. The difference is just that sometimes the changes don't bother us; we may even welcome them. Other times, we wish we could change history. This was one of those.

Larry and I had just gotten home from work when the call from Meredith came. I answered the phone and she asked me if Larry was home too. When I answered yes, she asked if we could both get on a phone. At that point the shaking began, the uncontrollable tremble of fear.

"It's cancer," she said.

I was sitting on the side of my bed, on the quilt that had been made for us by my friend's mom for our wedding. My husband, on the cordless, came in to sit beside me.

There is something inside a person that takes over when the rest of you is falling apart. Without digesting the diagnosis, I asked what we would do next.

Meredith began to tell of the procedures.

"We'll need to do testing to find out how far it has gone," she began. She talked of speaking with a surgeon and an oncologist. We talked about telling Troy, currently a flight surgeon in the Air Force, and having him in on decisions, though he is miles away in Texas. At the end of the conversation Meredith told me that she knew yesterday, but she thought it might be better to give us one more normal day.

Larry got to make the toughest phone call of his life that night. He called my mom to tell her that I had cancer while I sat next to him on the couch and listened. I couldn't do it. I don't know why. I tell my mom most everything, but I couldn't tell her this.

It was Thursday, December 10, 1998.

The next week was a mix of testing, of working, of crying. I felt caught between worlds as I tried to finish up my job when it was the last thing on my mind. My boss was not quite as sentimental or understanding. She wanted to know when my reports would be ready to turn over to the person taking my place and how I could finish if I wasn't coming in to work. We were on the phone, as I sat on my living room floor with papers all around me, trying to sort things out. I was shocked at the insensitivity, but it was a quick lesson that the world went on even when your life was falling apart.

One day I met with a surgeon, a nice middle-aged man who was talking to Troy as I was in his office. I learned that surgery would likely be the first step to remove the tumor that measured 5 centimeters. I learned that 5 centimeters was huge, in terms of tumors. He also taught me about the stages of breast cancer and quoted survival statistics at each stage. By the time he got to stage IV he shook his head and said those weren't so good.

This kind doctor also gave me pamphlets to read about cancer. You get diagnosed with a life threatening disease and you get pamphlets. They were about cancer, chemotherapy and radiation. I found the information inside discouraging.

After leaving his office Larry and I went back to the hospital to meet Meredith and her husband Chad, also a doctor. They wanted to pray with us, and along with two other doctors we found a quiet conference room on an upper floor of the hospital.

I had never prayed like that before, even with a lifetime of Sundays at church under my belt. It started with a scripture read by Chad, and then, with me sitting in a chair in the middle, everyone placed a hand on me. They prayed for complete healing and for protection for our family and me. They prayed for strength and direction, for good doctors and long life. It was deeply touching to have strangers pour their hearts out to God on my behalf.

We left that night feeling a bit better, a bit more prepared to fight.

I continued on my journey of tests. I was having a bone scan, the big test to determine whether or not the cancer has spread to my bones. Up until that point we still held hope that it wasn't too serious, that I was still in the good percentages that the surgeon had spoken of. I laid on the table in one of those ridiculous hospital gowns that three of my closest friends could have fit into with me. It was chilly and uncomfortable, although its design reminded me of a tanning bed. With the top closed down you can lay your head to the side and watch all sorts of people scurrying around. There is no privacy, however, as the tech that was administering my test didn't bother to pull the curtain that separates me from the main hall.

I was already edgy before we got started. It was late in the afternoon and they were running behind. I still had my first meeting with an oncologist that day, and I wasn't sure that we would make it. To top that off

I had to sit in a cramped waiting room full of pregnant women, and their husbands, all awaiting ultrasounds. My husband and I were awaiting news of how far the cancer had spread. I was not impressed with the hospital design at that moment as they rubbed their big bellies and smiled.

As my scan finished the tech said, "We'd like you to go to x-ray to have some pictures done."

"No," I said, "I've already been there; I need to get to my oncology appointment."

"I know," she told me. "We'll let them know that you'll be a little late; we need some more pictures."

"Is there something wrong?" I asked, wondering if the shaking is from fear or cold.

Without answering she told me that x-ray was down the hall on the left.

Oh my God. I walked out to Larry, the familiar tears welling up in my eyes. I was quite a sight I'm sure, standing in my enormous gown, holding the back shut with one hand, and telling him in a quivering voice that they want more X-rays.

"Okay," my tower of strength said. "It's okay; maybe they just didn't get what they needed."

"Or maybe it's everywhere!" I burst out and then began to crumple into him.

Slowly I told him that I could see the screen during the test, that I saw a bunch of spots in different

17

places. I didn't know what they were, but I had a pretty good guess. He gathered me up and held me for a minute, rubbing my back, running his fingers through my hair. He lets his touch be my comfort, knowing that there are no words for this situation that we were in. When he knew I was recovering he asked if I was ready. I give him a nod and off we went, down the hall and to the left.

This tech was a politician too, smiling when he thought it was appropriate, avoiding all of my questions, and going for small talk instead. He ushered me back into his room, big and cold with metal gleaming all around. I asked him about the views he's taking, and after a few vague non-answers on his part I realized he wouldn't talk about what I wanted to talk about. Clamming up, I turned when he told me to and waited for the okay to put my clothes back on and regain just a little dignity.

I wondered if the downward spiral was ever going to end as we drove to the oncology appointment.

We arrived at his office late, with films in hand. After giving them to the receptionist we took a seat in the large waiting room. Cancer must be a big business. I don't recall any conversation. What was left to say?

After a while Larry and I were put in an exam room and the doctor appeared. He was taller than us, probably close to 6 feet or more. His tone was sullen if not a bit angry. He was difficult from the start, wanting to know if Meredith had told us the results of the bone scan. We explained that the scan was just done, and then we came directly to him. After hearing that he left us, to call her, I found out later.

A few minutes passed and he reappeared, telling us that this wasn't his job, that my doctor should be telling me the results of my tests. By that time I was completely frazzled, though my outward appearance was one of unshakable composure. After a bit more hemming and hawing he began his dismal picture, still disgusted that he was the one giving me the news.

"The cancer, I'm afraid, is in your bones. Once it leaves its primary site and begins to travel it's quite difficult to control. We can try some chemo, but I wouldn't make any promises."

It hit me that he meant I had stage IV cancer. It had progressed so far that the percentages were dismal enough to make the surgeon I had met just shake his head rather than quote them to me. Now they were talking about me.

I'll never forget my next words, nor will Larry as he was feeling as though he had been punched in the stomach and he couldn't believe how evenly I fired them out.

From my spot on the exam table I looked down at the doctor sitting in a chair.

"I'm 26 years old and that's the best you can do for me?"

He nodded his head slowly. He thought that was the best he could do. He did know of a colleague who was doing this very experimental stem cell procedure that he might be able to call. He thought it would be best though if I got my affairs in order right away and that we begin chemotherapy as soon as he got back from his skiing trip.

SKIING!!! I was dying, and he had the nerve to tell me he was going skiing. I had never been so low. He proceeded to show us the chemotherapy area and hand me some more pamphlets. I was getting quite a collection by then. He explained that the nurse that ran this area would call and set things up with me. We left the office to walk into a cold, dark night. It matched my thoughts perfectly. That night's ride home seemed to take hours.

There wasn't much to be said. I was defeated. We went home and I called my mom, telling her it didn't look good.

December 17, 1998, had become the worst day of my life.

Lying in bed that night I asked Larry if he was scared to be alone. His response broke my heart.

"I'm not scared to be alone; I'm scared to be without you."

Don't Quit

When things go wrong as they
sometimes will,
When the road you're trudging seems
all up hill,
When funds are low, and debts are
high,
And you want to smile, but you have
to sigh,
When care is pressing you down a bit,
Rest if you must, but don't you quit.

Success is failure turned inside out,
The silver tint of the clouds of
doubt,
And you never can tell how close you
are,
It may be near when it seems afar.
So, stick to the fight when you are
hardest hit-
It's when things go wrong that you
mustn't quit.

- Author Unknown

3. Hope

Sydney Bs,

    I can't wait to bake cookies with you. I want to be able to go shopping together, and to watch you sing in a Christmas program. I am going to do those things; nobody else can be there like I can. How can cancer take away my time with you? Doesn't it realize you need me? I know you can't answer that; sometimes you just have to ask. Do you know how I met Daddy? It was at a summer camp where I was working. He came with Uncle Rob to chaperone kids. He wasn't much help though; as soon as we met he spent all of his time with me and my friend, Katie. We enjoyed being together from the start; there is nobody that I would rather be with. I hope you find someone like that someday. I love you Syd.

Mommy

Larry went to work the next day, the Friday before Christmas break. He'd already missed a couple of days, and it looked as though he would be missing more. I stayed home with Sydney, moping, not knowing what to do. It was strange. I felt fine, but I was dying? I thought that's what the doctor told me yesterday.

I turned on the TV to try to take my mind off the craziness of my life. It only intensified it. How could people be clapping and cheering on The Price is Right? Didn't they know what was happening to me? I felt as though I couldn't fit in to my own life anymore.

Sydney, having just celebrated her first birthday a few months ago was becoming more of a little person each day. Thankfully, she seems oblivious to all the changes in our lives. Her needs remain the same. In some ways that is comforting. She just expects me to take care of her.

Mid-morning my friend Marnie calls. Marnie is my PT counterpart. She worked in the same schools as I did and saw a lot of the same kids. Marnie was the one who showed me around most of the buildings when I started, and we had been developing a friendship as we worked together. We could talk for hours about anything, and I found myself looking forward to the days we would be working in the same building on the same day. We are night and day in many ways. She's tall and willowy with blond hair and blue eyes, and I stand a stockier

5'5" with dark hair and hazel eyes. Marnie was in the band in high school. I was an athlete. But there was an understanding between us even without words and we shared a mutual faith in God. This morning we cried together.

"I've still got so much I need to tell her," I sobbed into the phone. I am sitting on the bottom step of the stairs, head down, feeling as though I am crumpling into the floor. I had just seen a program where a dying mother made videos for her children. I wondered if I'd be doing the same.

Marnie, a mom of two angels of her own, croons, "I know, I know. We'll take care of that if we need to."

She gave me an honest answer, admitting to me that this was a serious battle that I was beginning.

"I am praying for complete healing, she told me; I haven't always done that in the past for others. I may pray for strength or for God's will, but this time I believe it is right to ask for healing." Go, Marn, go. Pray away.

She gave me strength to carry on, and after a long conversation I decided to pack up Sydney and travel the 50 minutes of back roads to get to her house. Marnie had troubles of her own right then. Two days before my initial diagnosis she fell and broke her leg. The two bones below the knee snapped, both of them clean through. Marn was housebound for a while, a virtual blessing in *disguise. I needed her to be there for me. God saw to it that it happened.*

Marnie's house is always a bit like a circus. This morning when I arrived her kids are running around while her mom was trying to get lunch together. Mike, her husband, came in to check on things and headed back to work on the farm where they live.

The dining room is the center of the house and all the activity goes on around it. There is a constant motion of kids and daily life. It was nice to be engulfed in the sound of voices; it'd been rather quiet at my house lately. Rather than feel awkward upon arrival you just become another part of the motion. Before I know it Sydney is entertained and Marnie and I are sitting and talking over a stir-fry dish that a friend had brought over to her, the invalid.

I told her about my visit at the doctor's the day before and how dismal it was. Then I told her that I called my mom who in turn called my brother Troy. She told him that this was not acceptable, that they needed to do something. Troy dropped everything in Texas and got to work on being a big brother.

First he talked with Meredith, and they decided that U of M, where they had gone to medical school was the best place to start. Next he called a doctor who he had worked with and asked him who the best was for fighting breast cancer. He was given the name of Dr. Sofia

Merajver, and he proceeded to track her down in her lab. Troy gave her all the information that he had and she responded by telling him, she's a U of M patient.

Troy called me at Marnie's a bit later and told me she would be calling. I hadn't left my house without calling my mom and Larry to tell them where I was going so there was no trouble tracking me down. Within the hour she did call.

Her accent made it difficult for me to hear everything with all of the noise our kids were creating. I stole away to a quiet room and began to answer her questions. They were not about the cancer; they were about me, my family, and my life. We began talking about the different ways of killing cancer. After a lot of reassurance Dr. Merajver gave me her home phone number and some instructions for the weekend.

"Start drinking green tea, eat lots of fruit and veggies, and we'll start killing cancer on Monday."

On Monday? Not after Christmas? Not after skiing? Oh no. We were already killing cancer; she just gave me the okay to fight.

I hung up the phone and walked out to Marn, not quite believing that it had all happened. Her home phone number? Do doctors do that?

It was the first glimpse of hope that I'd seen in a week. Like a breath of fresh air it revitalized me, helped me to stand up straight and move forward. I don't think Dr. Merajver could ever know how much that conversation mattered to me.

Still in shock I began to tell Marnie about the conversation.

"She asked about me and my job. She wanted to know how old Sydney was. She asked about Larry and whether or not we had a good marriage. It was a long time before we even talked about the cancer. She's so much better. I'm going on Monday."

Marnie just listened to me, relieved to see a ray of hope.

The prayer that had been prayed that night with Meredith to bring the right doctor into my life had been answered. I was sure of it.

And so, I decided I needed to live my life, whatever was left of it. We had tickets to an Amy Grant Christmas program for the next night. Larry and I were supposed to go with a group of people from our church. Marnie and her husband Mike were supposed to go too. Mike had gotten tickets long before Marnie's spill on the front porch.

I knew I couldn't face a group of people yet. The reaction of the few people that I had seen since my diagnosis was to cry, which made me cry. Since Marnie and I had already put that behind us I thought it might be okay to go to the concert together. We planned to meet at her house the next day.

The drive down was uneventful, but the conversation was difficult. It is hard to make small talk with someone who has just been diagnosed with cancer. Larry and Mike talked about skiing, a common interest. I sat quietly and turned everything said into something about cancer. I wondered if I could ever plan a trip again, or if Larry would have to take them without me someday.

After dinner at the restaurant next door we headed to the arena for the concert. Larry and Mike had gone over early and sweet-talked an usher to let us in to handicapped seating on account of Marnie's wheelchair. The seats were good, the music was good, my ability to cope was not good. I listened with tears sliding down my cheeks. I couldn't fight off the thoughts of not seeing my daughter grow, of making my husband a widow before he turned 30, of how good it was for everyone else at the concert just celebrating another Christmas.

I had spotted our group from church soon after we were seated. They were way up high, to the left of the stage. The thought of facing them sapped all of my strength. I had never been great at handling other peoples' emotions, and now they were because of me. At the intermission Larry asked if I wanted to go up there. I didn't, but I did. I walked the steps to the top and waited for the reaction. There were hugs mainly and some talk of how much better our seats were. It was the idle conversation that I was becoming used to, because no one knew how to make this better. It was all helpful though and upon returning to our seats Marnie said I looked as though a weight had been lifted from my shoulders. I had faced the first group of people, and now I could face more. I actually even sang a little during the second part of the concert, my terrible voice right next to Marnie's beautiful one.

Don't be afraid to take a big step if

one is indicated.

You can't cross a chasm is two small

jumps.

David L. George

4. Amaizin' Blue

Sydney Bs

    We make plans all of the time. We're going to do this and then that and on and on. I had made all those plans, and they were moving along rather smoothly. And then in a day it changes. That is why everyday is so important. Everyday you can make a difference in the way that your day goes. You can shrug off an angry person, or you can get angry too. You can make someone else's day by smiling. In this world that seems to be all about stuff, it isn't that at all. It's about people. There is nothing better than the sound of your all out belly laugh. I smile thinking of it. Or being on the couch, you, me, and Daddy. That is it, heaven on earth. I treasure you more everyday.

Loving you,

Mommy

Larry, my mom, and I set out early Monday morning to find Dr. Merajver. Armed with maps from the internet and directions that Troy had given us over the phone we wound our way through the hills and curves and one way streets of Ann Arbor to find ourselves in front of a rounded glass building tucked in behind the main hospital. As luck would have it, it even had its own parking ramp adjoining. As we pulled in we were greeted with a computer generated female voice welcoming us to the University of Michigan's Comprehensive Cancer and Geriatrics Center. The name and building were impressive, and a bit intimidating.

The entrance to the cancer center was a large revolving glass door. Five people could easily fit into each of its compartments. It moved quite slowly, making you shuffle your feet to move forward. There was a soft whoosh whoosh sound every twenty seconds or so as it sealed and resealed again. I've come to believe that the slow entrance to the cancer center is almost symbolic, a time to reflect on the life that is your own. Once you have entered it may never be the same again.

Once inside we began to learn the ropes. First and foremost a hospital blue card. On the main floor of the center we sat down with a receptionist who gathered all of our information about employment, insurance, and next of kin. She then produced a credit card in U of M blue. This would be something that everyone would ask for at every desk in the hospital. With it a person could tell just about anything including what appointments are scheduled and what labs need to be drawn. "Have you got your blue card?" had to be one of the most common questions asked on a daily basis.

Our next stop was 50 feet to the left of the main reception desk, the blood draw station, a.k.a. the vampires. It is a respectful term; there is nobody better at getting blood than these people, even from disappearing veins. A woman asked for my card and told me she would call me when it was my turn. A chance to sit down gave me the opportunity to look around. It was a large space with lots of open air. The blood draw area separated itself with partitions rather than walls allowing all the areas of the main floor to be separate and yet together. It was a cornucopia of textures and life that made me wonder. There was the shiny gold trim that outlined furniture and ran down walls and partitions. At various locations there were small sculpture art pieces encapsulated in glass. The furniture was upholstered in a tweedy fabric, and chairs and love seats were gathered together in small groups to achieve a homey affect.

The amazing thing however, was the people. Young children with their parents, old people with their children. Some look frightenly ill, others as fit as marathon runners. It was hard not to wonder if cancer brought each of them here, and if they would survive.

I didn't feel as though I fit in with any of them. You could tell that many were regulars by the way they greeted and were greeted by the staff.

"How are you doing today?" followed by, "Wow your hair is growing again!" This was normal conversation within these walls.

After an easy blood draw of eight or so tubes I was sent upstairs to meet my doctor.

Mondays are Breast Clinic days at U of M, and the waiting area, which could seat 75 people, was packed. After signing in and leaving all of the films that I brought with the receptionist, I waited my turn. I had no expectations for being seen quickly as I knew I had been squeezed in. Once again I looked around, never knowing that so many people dealt with breast cancer and realizing that I was easily younger than all of them.

My name was called, my vital statistics taken, and we were all ushered into one of many examining rooms. Before long Ginny strolled in, making me feel at ease instantly. Her title was nurse practitioner but her mannerism was that of Sue, my best friend's mom. She was short with graying hair, an easy smile, and a concerned but confident tone. After giving her a synopsis of the last week, which had turned my world upside down, she left to go and get Dr. Merajver. It surprised me that she handled it all so easily, as if 26 year olds with stage IV cancer come her way all the time.

*"Heather? I am Sofia Merajver, how are you doing?"
The words were a bit clipped, an accent, which I had
heard in my phone conversation.*

*After a brief introduction of my mom and Larry
we began to talk of the cancer. The discussion helped
us to understand each other better. I made it clear
that I was going to fight, and I needed someone to help
me. Sofia told me that I was strong and that we could
be aggressive in attacking the cancer or we could just
try to extend my life and make me comfortable while the
cancer took over.*

*"Cancer does not scare me," she said. "I see how
it works. It can be tricky, but we will fight it."*

*I did not even hear the part about just trying to
extend my life; I was there to get rid of the cancer.
I told Dr. Merjaver that I had heard enough bad stuff
that I only wanted to hear positive things. I wasn't
even interested in knowing all of the places that it
had spread to in my bones. I knew it would only make me
feel worse.*

*Dr. Merjaver was okay with those things but she
said we needed to make sure that it hadn't gone anywhere
else and so she would order a few more tests. A CAT
scan of my brain, to be sure there was no cancer on it,
and a MRI to get a good look at all of my organs. The
prospect of more tests made me shiver. Every test that I
had taken since being diagnosed had been bad, revealing*

more cancer and grimmer chances. I didn't think I could handle much more bad news. After all, less than two weeks ago my life was normal.

The question of children was raised.

"You have a daughter right? Did you plan on having more?"

Larry and I looked at each other and then I mumbled that we didn't know.

My mom answered for us. "You had planned on having more than one child," she said.

"Yes," I answered. "We did."

She told us that it would not be good for me to get pregnant, and answered my question about doing so in the future with a we'll have to see.

In a time span of less than two minutes my dream of more children was replaced with killing cancer as matter of factly as stating that the sky is blue. This was a whole new ball game from my previous life. It was about facts and not feelings. No time to feel sorry. We had things to do. Feeling sorry could come later.

She then began to talk of the course of treatment which we would be starting on right away and I began to learn the words that would become a regular part of my vocabulary. It was a world that I knew nothing of and I was engulfed in it. Gone were the days of idle conversation.

We spoke first of chemotherapy, and of the drugs which she felt would be the most effective. I would use two drugs initially, Adriomyacin and Taxotere. Dr. Merjaver instilled confidence in the drugs as she talked, leading me to believe that they could take on anything. After four rounds of this regiment we could possibly do a stem cell transplant, a newer procedure, which uses high dose chemotherapy first, and then stem cells to reintroduce life to my body. Surgery and radiation were also possibilities.

It was amazing really. I felt as though I had more options than I might even need to take on the cancer. A couple of days ago I hadn't had any.

She did a physical examination. If she was shocked at the size of the tumor, I never knew. Instead she reassured me that finding it would have been difficult given the location behind the nipple and the changes with pregnancy, and breast-feeding.

After the exam Dr. Merjaver left to get Kelly, the nurse who completed her team. Kelly entered with an easy but professional manner. She looked to be in her late twenties, a fit person with short auburn hair. Kelly exuded capability and after a quick introduction and a bit of joking with Dr. Merjaver she walked me through the handful of prescriptions that she held in her hand. Drugs to help with nausea after the chemo, a series of shots that I would give myself to help with my white *blood count, and drugs to take before I came for chemo again in three weeks. She also gave me phone number upon phone number so that I could always get in touch with her. No subject was off limits, from my sex life to my hair falling out. Kelly informed me that it would happen two weeks to the day after my first chemo session. Before leaving the room to take me down to the infusion area to start my chemo Kelly gave me a hug and said words that I will never forget. You're my age; we're not going to lose you.*

In meeting Ginny, Dr. Merajver, and Kelly I was given a lifeboat. I knew the sea was stormy but at least I had some way of getting to the shore. The talk of death was left with the doctor who was skiing right now. I had so much confidence in each of them. They were all more knowledgeable and approachable than I ever could have imagined. The best of the best. I didn't doubt that for a second. I understood a little bit more about the arrogance that surrounded U of M. I felt they had earned it.

And so, we went down to the infusion area. I was finding that everywhere we went the activity level was on high, an intermingling of separate doctors and services all together creating one loud hum. Having only seen the small infusion area at the first oncologist's office I was amazed at the scene here. We walked down a short hallway with a kitchenette on the right. It was stocked with various drinks and snacks, and was available to all patients during treatment. The hallway then opened up as it followed a circular path to the left. On the left were reclining chairs, one after another and approximately thirty in all. I realized that we were inside the rounded glass that I saw from the outside. In the chairs were the people getting their chemo with family and friends sitting close by in less comfortable chairs. There were IV poles at each recliner, and TV's for every two chairs. It was a busy area, yet very low-key. Some people were talking, others sleeping. All were fighting cancer.

Off of the recliner wing, behind the kitchenette was a smaller circle that had individual rooms with beds in them. They were for the people who were really sick, or for rookies like me. I was shown to a room with a view and we settled in with me in the bed and Mom and Larry sitting along side. We turned on the TV and waited for my nurse.

I couldn't recall a lot of nurses that I encountered, but I will never forget Marlene. I liked her instantly, as did Larry and my mom. It can't be easy to put a family at ease during a first chemo session, but Marlene did that for us, and we will always be grateful.

I began with an IV in my arm and fluids going in. Marlene put on her gown and gloves and then she hooked a bag of the taxotere to my pole. She told me she would start it slowly. I was to tell her if I wasn't feeling well or I felt like I couldn't breathe. In it went and almost immediately the feeling of nausea swept over me along with a warmth that crawled right up to my ears. Marlene was watching and backed it off, it was a reaction she said, and I was having a reaction.

Up to this point all I knew about chemo I had learned from TV or books. It made a person throw up a lot. They lost their hair. Kelly had already told me that I would be losing my locks so I assumed the throwing up part was also true. I thought that what was happening was normal. Marlene assured me that it wasn't.

After taking more Decadron and Benadryl to stop a reaction we tried again. This time there was nothing, and in it flowed to go and find the cancer and destroy it. It took one and one half hours to do the Taxotere. When it was complete we moved on to Adriomyocin. The red devil Marlene told me they called it that because it was red and so strong. I loved the name, and the fact that it was tough as nails. My cancer didn't stand a chance. After five minutes it was in and I was done. I walked out looking the same as I did when I entered, but I was not the same.

I felt the need to tell everyone what was going on. Our news was spreading quickly and we were in the midst of uncomfortable conversations with everyone. One night one of Larry's friends called after having found out.

I answered the phone and he asked to speak with Larry not knowing what to say to me. He was one of many, so I wrote the following letter.

Dear Friends,

     I am writing this letter to tell you that we have a mountain to climb, and we would appreciate your help. The past week has been amazing, but enlightening. On Thursday evening I got a call from my doctor to tell me that I have breast cancer. What a big word! We are in the midst of doing numerous tests and charting a course for treatment. It is definite that I will begin chemo soon, and will have a mastectomy later. We have all agreed that it will be treated aggressively, though it won't be pleasant. Please don't feel sorry for me. Cry if you need to, I certainly do, but after that please decide to make a difference. We need your prayers. God says in James 5: 13-16 Is any one of you in trouble? He should pray. Is anyone happy? He should sing songs of praise. Is any one of you sick? He should call the elders of the church to pray over him and anoint him with oil in the name of the Lord. And the person offered in faith will make the sick person well: The Lord will raise him up. Therefore confess your sins to each other and pray for each other so that you may be healed. The prayer of a righteous man is powerful and effective. If you wonder if you can make a difference we know that you can. Matthew 17:20 says Because you have so little faith. I tell you the truth, if you have the faith as small as a mustard seed, you can say to this mountain, Move from here to there and it will move. Nothing will be impossible for you. Aside from praying, I would like to be kept in the loop of a normal life. I would love to have lots of mail of encouragement, inspiring, funny and everyday life. Tell us if you saw a good movie. We may be renting a few. Talk to us about real things and insignificant things, I'm sure we'll need it. We are setting up spokespeople to help us coordinate the things that we may need so that if you wanted news on me or to offer assistance they could help you. We will also be online before the beginning of the New Year; maybe I'll become a computer geek.

I am smiling right now. I have a great family and we're going to fight. We are not saying why me? Rather we are saying try me! We can do this, please help lift us up. God's will be done a lot of people are going to come out of our trials with a stronger faith, us included.

God Bless You,

Heather & Larry

I don't know where the words came from, but I know they touched many. The letter began to circulate from friends to people we had never met.

Trust in God and do something.

-Mary Lyon

5. Beginnings and Endings

Sydney Bs

My job is to protect you, to care for you, to help you grow up. And then I'm diagnosed and I'm not sure that I can do that. Something you could never understand is going to impact every part of your life. That isn't fair to you, but life certainly isn't about fair.

We are each going to be better and stronger in the end. For now though please understand that mommy isn't going to be feeling very well all of the time, and that playing may not be a priority. You'll probably be with Daddy, Nana, and Grandma more than with me for a while, but we'll make it, and we'll savor every moment that we can.

God is with us. The doctors prayed with me after being diagnosed, seeking healing and restoration for my body. It is time to expect a miracle

Love you,

Mommy

After I left U of M I began to bolster my strength, be presented with resources, and deal with the emotions that others were feeling. Looking back, the last two weeks of December, Christmas vacation, was a dark time of muddling through.

Meredith had given me the name and phone number of her aunt, a doctor who was a breast cancer survivor in California. Meredith told me that she had made a lot of changes in her diet and believed that it had really made a difference. I called her one evening from my parents' house. Armed with a pen and legal pad I began to learn of things that I could do to kill cancer. By the time I hung up I had a pad full of scribbles indicating that I needed to dramatically change the way that I ate. It was a bit overwhelming as she talked about meat, dairy, sugar, and white flour all being things that feed cancer as opposed to vegetables, fruits and whole grains which could reverse the disease process. I knew that I had a lot of work and research to do, but I was so grateful to have something that I could control and participate in.

My mom immediately offered to research. She has always been good at that kind of thing. One of her friends had told her that it was important that someone other than the patient do the research, as you have to shlep through a lot of dismal information to get to the good stuff. She had been doing that for her son's battle with Leukemia and he had pulled through a terrible battle. The good stuff can be lifesaving, and the medical community knows that you are participating fully.

I did well after my chemo treatment; the drugs that Kelly had given me addressed virtually every problem from an upset stomach to a head full of thoughts that wouldn't slow down. My prayer journal describes it a bit better.

Dear Lord,

This is a journey, a new one that I never expected. Cancer, not just a little bit, metastatic breast cancer, cancer in my bones. I feel healthy; I guess I'm not. I've had my diagnosis for 2 weeks now. Is it sinking in? I'm not sure, but it is always there. Last night I tried to sleep without drugs since chemo. It was not very restful, but I made it. Thank you for no strange racing thoughts, they are so bothersome. I'm not sure how to feel Lord. I trust you, I know how to fight. Do I just go on? Am I suppose to be reflecting on all of this and making something good happen? I don't know. Thank you for my life. I have a beautiful daughter that screeches and smiles for everyone. Help me to stay close to her, for her to want her Mommy even if she is sick. Thank you for a husband whose commitment is stronger than I know. Please strengthen him. Thank you for a mom who is willing to have us all stay for as long as we need to. Lord, help me to focus on today- it doesn't seem so big then.

One night we went to a neighborhood Christmas party. It was a small gathering, mainly two families that I had grown up with. I wasn't keeping in touch the way they had, so I had lost that comfortable feeling of just hanging out. Add to that cancer and everyone was uncomfortable. Thank God for kids. They always provide entertainment and something to talk about. My closest friend growing up was there that night. Christy and I had racked up many hours as children doing all sorts of things from playing with dolls, to riding our dirt bikes, to swimming in the pool. In high school we hung with a large group of friends. Christy, being two years my senior, let me drive long before anyone else, and provided me with my first college experiences. We had both gotten married within a year and moved in separate directions. Since that time the phone calls had dwindled to a couple of times per year.

And so, when Christy told me that she had just quit her job and would be able to do anything I needed I didn't believe her. I had been hearing empty offers for some time already from all sorts of people. It is just what people say when they hear of something tragic. I just nodded and said okay and we went on with the night.

I honestly don't remember Christmas that year except for the fact that our family was in different places. My mom and dad had made plans to go to Texas to visit family. With all that was going on I asked my mom to stay home, which she did and my dad went with my brother and grandparents. They spent a lot of time praying in dismal Brownsville, Texas.

I began to search for hope. One day my mom and I went to the Christian bookstore to find anything on the subject. She, in her grief, had said she would buy me any book I wanted. The selection was not great. Though I could find many books about cancer they were so discouraging I couldn't read them. The one book I found to be helpful was Chicken Soup for the Surviving Soul. It spoke about conquering a lot of things, and conquering was something I wanted to know more about.

I bought a red spiral bound notebook to use as a journal of some sort. I picked red because it is bold and feisty. It was always my favorite color. On the front cover I listed my name and address in case I left it somewhere. Under that I put a column for answered prayers. I wanted to be able to remind myself of God's hand in this. I began by listing U of M and Dr. Merajver. It went everywhere with me.

Mom and I also shopped for a wig. I wasn't sure that I would ever wear it, but I wanted the option. Before my hair came out I wanted to shop, so they would know what it was supposed to look like. The ladies in the shop were nice, though a little too sweet for me. By the end I was just glad it was done. I was feeling sorry for myself, asking why I should have to be the one shopping for a wig.

As the Christmas season ended I faced my first day on my new job. I knew that I wouldn't be working while doing chemo; I had too many other things to work on. I waited anxiously to go back on the Monday after break and than, because of bad weather, it was canceled. This wouldn't have been a problem except for the fact that Kelly had said that my hair would fall out in two weeks, which was Monday, and she was right on the money. I could reach up and pull just a little and out it came. I resisted as I wanted to look okay for my first day.

I went to work on Tuesday, spending the first minutes explaining to my new boss that I needed to work one day to continue benefits. He said he could ask for a leave through the end of the school year. Being a brand new employee he thought they would grant that, but if I couldn't return by September my job would be gone. It was a hard, hard day. I worked in a preschool classroom, basically as an aide. I made small talk with people I had never met before trying to avoid the whole issue of cancer that would only make me cry. As I drove home I tugged at the hair on my head pulling out handfuls of my thick dark brown hair.

By the time I was home I was so glad to be done. I wasn't a normal person anymore; I couldn't do normal things as if there wasn't cancer. When Larry got home I *told him I couldn't watch my hair fall out, and so we went to work on it. It actually was a bonding experience. We tried scissors, and than clippers, and finally a razor to shave my head smooth. My husband can find the humor in anything and by the time we were done he said, you look great, making me feel much better. The shocking thing was it didn't look that bad to me. So I found a bandana, put it on and off we went, to a basketball game at the high school.*

The transformation was being made inwardly and outwardly. I began to realize that I was a cancer battler. It needed to be who I was- the most important job in my life.

I never ended up using the wig I had purchased. It felt phony to me, an aid to be used to make someone comfortable. If I had a wig on a person might not even know that I had cancer, and that was the largest part of my life. I chose to deal with an occasional stare with the hope that people would accept me as I was.

If

I could

sit

across

the porch

from

God

I'd thank

Him

for

lending me

you.

-Flavia

6. Angels Among Us

Sydney Bs,

A fresh new day is a gift, though I never realized it before. Enjoying that day is our responsibility, a way of using the gift given to us. As a little one you are so good at enjoying things, delighted in a face that Daddy makes or throwing you up into the air. Everyday more words are coming out of your mouth, it is amazing. It is so good to be with you, I guess I need to thank the cancer for that, for being at home to see your smile. We are making it hon; there are lots of people wanting to help us. Keep smiling.

Mommy

We began a new routine, one of fighting cancer and dealing with the roller coaster of thoughts that would run through my head. One moment I would be sure I was killing cancer and than a little ache would make me unsure of myself again. I added another doctor to my team. From the very beginning Dr. Merjaver had spoken of a stem cell procedure, and she referred me to Dr. Lois Ayash. For all of Dr. Merjaver's exuberance Dr. Ayash was very reserved, for all of Dr. Merjaver's words of encouragement Dr. Ayash offered words of caution.

We met on a chemo day in an exam room down the hall from Dr. Meravjer. We had been told that the stem cell procedure was pretty involved and that we should feel free to bring a tape recorder to record the conversation. My mom and Larry were with me as usual.

The content of our conversation was fairly one-sided with Dr. Ayash laying out the procedure, the potential problems and the statistics to this point. More testing would be needed to determine whether or not I would be a candidate.

I found myself really liking Dr. Ayash, and having confidence in her. I wanted her to believe in me also, and made it a goal to be one of her good statistics. When I told her as much, I got a small smile in return, spurring me forward. At home I added her to my answered prayer column in my red noteook. My second letter was written and went out to a larger group than the first.

Dear Friends,

Thank you for your faithfulness as we embark on the journey of a lifetime. Your support has been incredible. It has been wonderful to hear from new and old friends as well as people committed to help us just because they feel they are being called to do so.

I am doing great! I am feeling well, though that cycles a bit with chemo. I have yet to actually be sick though, Praise God. My spirit is soaring. I believe that God wants me to live and live I shall. I am in the process of making some changes in my life. I have cut out meat and dairy products and am working with a nutritionist at the Cancer Center to find the best diet to starve my cancer. I have also been talking with people and finding some vitamins and herbs that are being consistently recommended. We have found that we have some very knowledgeable people right in our community to help us. The information that you all have sent has been invaluable and we would ask that you continue to research for us.

In the medical realm I have completed 2 of 4 chemo sessions. The sessions happen on Mondays. On those days we spend the morning seeing my doc and then go to infusion where they give chemo through a needle in my arm. The people are wonderful. Sometime after my next session I will be doing a bone morrow biopsy to determine if there is cancer in my bone marrow. This is big. If there is no cancer we will be able to proceed with a stem cell transplant in Ann Arbor. If there are still cancer cells present we will need to go to one of a few centers in the country where they can separate the cancer cells out before giving my stem cells back to me. This whole process allows the doctors to give me very high levels of chemo to stop the cancer and then give me life by reintroducing the cells I need to fight infection, etc. I also have a CT scan upcoming to rule out cancer on my brain. Please pray that these tests come back negative, without cancer.

I wanted to let you know that God has answered prayers everyday for us. I was granted an extended medical leave at my new job; He directed my brother Troy to great doctors at U of M; Larry's aunt gave us a computer; I look good bald (you never know about the shape of your head); Sydney is at her funniest and most spirited, learning and laughing everyday. Finally He has given us you, and everyday someone different bolsters my spirits.

The day after I was diagnosed in December my general doctor Meredith Furness, her husband Chad who is also a doc and three other doctors at St. Mary's prayed with us. Chad read a scripture in James 5 about healing. Since then I've been provided with many more. I'll leave you with another. Peace be with you, it is with me.

Heather & Larry

So you shall serve the Lord your God, and he will bless your bread and water. And I will take sickness away from the midst of you. Exodus 23:25

I call heaven and earth as witnesses today against you, that I have set before you life and death, blessing and cursing; therefore choose life, that both you and your descendants may live. Deuteronomy 30:19

People began to come forward with thoughts on my battle. I realized later that these were the angels among us. More often than not I had never met them but for one reason or another they reached out and joined in our fight.

I got a letter from Joanie who lives in Pittsburgh. Her daughter-in-law was a teacher at one of the schools that I worked at and she had told her about me. Joanie was a survivor of a similar diagnosis, and she had a wealth of information, which she shared wholeheartedly when I called her. She was very direct, telling me that I must make changes in my diet, pray, and get my mind fighting cancer. She was the first one to say with confidence, You can do this, I will pray for you, you will pray for me, and we will both be okay. Joanie had been through hell, in the midst of her treatment she woke up one morning to find her husband had died in his sleep. And yet she fought on with a determination that was clearly evident. Joanie traveled far and wide to find food that was good for her body, and she researched vitamins continually. She treated fighting cancer like a job, and was telling me that I must do so too. I was touched that a woman who didn't know me from Adam was so willing to help me. She invested a lot of time and energy encouraging me to take charge of my fight. She sent me Bernie Siegel tapes to listen to everyday to kill the cancer. It was amazing,

Heather Jose

and powerful.

Christy called back. It wasn't just to chat. She was asking what she could do or when would be a good time for her to come up. She said that she had told her husband Sean that this was a priority in her life, and she would be doing what she could for me. She came up a few days later, a two and a half hour drive in good weather. The friendship that was so much a part of our childhood began to surface again.

One day in talking with my pastor he told me that God had good things in store for me, that he really believed that. So I began to believe that too.

My schools that I had been working at were so kind. A large planter from the Sheridan Elementary staff arrived right after my diagnosis. Books and cards and little pick me ups came on a regular basis. Lakeview El provided gift certificates to the local pizza place so that Larry could stay fed.

The teachers at my husband's school were amazing, offering all kinds of support to him in terms of sick days and financial help if needed. It made it a nice place for him to go and to focus on things other than cancer. They were also very kind to me, as I was often up at school visiting. As I began to understand the importance of exercise the teacher who Larry had student taught for a couple of years previously offered to walk the halls with me. I would put Sydney in her stroller or leave her with Larry and off we would go.

My family offered different types of reassurance. Troy would tell me that the doctors were doing the very best treatment. I began to call him anytime something new was coming just to hear him tell me that he believed in it and that I could do it. It was a doctor perspective with a dose of big brother wisdom, a winning combination. Mom would tell me we would do whatever we needed to. Every day we talked, sometimes about big things other times not. Josh would just believe in me. And my dad would tell me that he loved me. Larry's family wanted to help out in any way possible, and Larry's mom and sister Kathy became Sydney's regular babysitter for all of our visits to Ann Arbor. Larry's sister Kim sent me a package from Minnesota where she lived. Included in it was a fountain with healing waters.

I'm not exactly sure how Pam came in to my life. She also taught school and attended our church, but I never knew her. Her husband Jim had died of cancer a few years ago. He was a teacher at the high school, a coach, loved by many. Pam was left with two school-age children to raise. Pam also believed in nutrition, positive thinking, and prayer. She offered me all sorts of resources in our very small community. Her spirit, which radiates from her, calmed me. She joined my group of believers, in me, in the ability to fight the battle with cancer. She told me that we would do anything we needed to, hire a chef, go see different doctors. Pam believed that Jim could also have survived if he had had the strength to fight by using diet, exercise and meditation. Pam always had encouraging words for me, words that had substance that led me forward in my fight.

One day I was feeling down, and a blue Toyota mini van pulled up to my house. Out of the van came Chris, with a small book and a chubby ceramic angel holding scripture for me. Chris grew up in the same small town that my husband did, and now lived in the same small town that we did some 100 miles away. She is a kindergarten teacher, with an easy smile and long straight brown hair, often drawn back in a loose bun. It is hard not to be cheered when in a conversation with her. The book was called Healed of Cancer by Dodie Osteen. It had been recommended to her by a friend. She wanted to help, and this is what she was led to do. The book had a profound effect on my thoughts, providing a spiritual basis to stand up to the cancer. It made me want to stand up and cheer. I read it constantly, wrote down all the verses in my red notebook, and read them some more. The red notebook became my healing notebook and I added everything that encouraged me.

My husband Larry was incredible. Always there to believe in me, he backed me in everything I did. As a coach he is a great encourager and that was so

reassuring. Above all, he treated me like
the humor in everything. That was the
could have done.

We also began a routine with some people ⌐⌐
church. We would get together and pray at my house.
Sometimes I would use my notebook to start us off and
then we would each take a turn praying for specific things
in my treatment, for my family, for healing. It was a
very powerful time, good for all involved I believe. I
learned that it was okay to ask God and other people for
specific things.

Though I felt as though I were doing things right I
always would wonder. Again God jumps in with reassurance.
This time it was sent by Kathy, my husband's aunt. Kathy
has this personality that draws people to her, a ray of
sunshine on the darkest of days. She lives in Ann Arbor
and one day while at church found herself talking with
Diana Dyer. Diana is a registered dietitian and three-
time cancer survivor. She had really researched food and
supplements to impact her fight. Out of the experience
she wrote a small book, which Kathy sent me with all
types of info, menus, shopping lists, and my favorite,
a shake recipe. The shake had soy, veggies, fruit, and
lots of other good stuff. It was a great way to start
your day. I took to it immediately.

The other book that accompanied this was by Greg
Anderson, a 15-year survivor of a 30 days to live

osis. His book was called <u>50 Essential Things To Do</u> <u>en The Doctor Says It's Cancer</u>. It was great for me. It laid out the plan that I was pursuing, good conventional medicine, time with God, exercise, nutrition, a purpose in life. He spoke of the healing notebooks he had filled on his journey. I drank it in. Every few chapters it would say take a break and I would be bummed. I wanted to consume it all.

Greg had started a group called the Cancer Conquerors (now the Cancer Recovery Foundation of America) and in the back of the book it told how you could become a member. I had grown to dislike the wishy-washy "do what you can approach" and was very interested in being a conqueror. The word resonated throughout my body. I joined right away. I was all for aligning myself with people who were taking on cancer head on, those who were not afraid to say I will fight.

The willingness of the people that were coming forward in my battle was amazing. I had someone to watch Sydney for a while everyday so that I could spend some intense time fighting cancer through prayer, exercise, and meditation. Lois, Sydney's adopted grandma, had been watching her most of her life. She continued to watch Syd, except now it was for free. I would have had meals everyday except that people no longer knew what I was eating.

My days began to settle down into a pattern. I

would get up in the morning and take Sydney and then return home. At home I would make a shake while listening to a "Songs for Life" CD. I would go for a walk, with my CD player in hand, knowing that God was in control, but wanting Him to want me to win this battle. There was a song on the CD; Warrior is a Child by Twila Paris that hit me hard. It speaks of appearing to be strong, winning battles left and right, but in reality being just a child, scared and at times tired. The time spent walking on my snow-covered dirt road was so good for me. It revived my body and my mind. I would come in and make a cup of hot green tea, read through all of my healing verses, and than lay down and listen to Bernie. Together we would target the cancer and make that area strong again. I could than make a good lunch and go and get my daughter.

There was a period initially when I struggled with sending Sydney away while I was at home. My outlook began to shift though, and I began to think of my time as something I was doing so that we could be together for a long time. Though she could have been home and I still could have made breakfast and taken her with me for a walk, the focus would have been different, on her needs rather than my own. The more I read, the more I realized that I needed to take care of myself, and do it well. It wasn't selfish, as we like to view in our society. It was necessary, and I was worth the investment. By spending time alone each day I could give the rest of my day to our family, without feeling that there were things that I should be doing to take care of myself. I laughed, however, as some people thought that I used my babysitting time to rest. That wasn't part of the schedule. I was busy telling my body that I was strong, and didn't need extra rest. Adequate, yes. Extra, no.

Today I gave all I had,

What I kept I've lost forever.

-Author Unknown

7. The Rest of the Puzzle

Sydney Bs,

You can do anything that you want to do. It probably won't be easy, but you can do it. Don't live in fear of failure. Stand up and plow through to get to your goal. I think we limit ourselves so much sometimes, because we don't think we can. You don't limit yourself right now. It doesn't matter if you fall down, you will still get back up and try again to reach the goal. And if you fall again, you'll get up again, knowing that the goal is worth the struggle. What a great quality. It seems a shame that we teach it away.

The words keep coming, and some of them break my heart. The other day you found an empty bottle that you held up with a question forming. "Mommy medicine?" you ask. Yes, Mommy's medicine, I wish you didn't have to know. I love you.

Mommy

The day came for my bone marrow biopsy. Dr. Ayash was doing the procedure. She told me it would be a bit uncomfortable as I didn't have a lot of cushion on my tush. She used a long needle to extract marrow from my pelvic bone on each side. It is an interesting thing to have someone leaning into you with all their strength, and I was glad that it was over.

As I got up I said, "It's going to come back clean."

Dr. Ayash, with a little smile, shook her head as if to say I hope so.

With many aspects of my treatment rolling along, chemo every third Monday, prayer meetings, regular exercise and meditation I found only one piece of the puzzle troubling. Nutrition, I knew it was very important, but the amount of information was staggering, everything from a strict macrobiotic diet to eat whatever you want, you need the calories.

Having spoken with Meredith's aunt and later with Joanie, I had an idea that a vegetarian lifestyle might be permanent. Reading Diana's book confirmed it, with the exception of fish. I did not have a problem with this, but I wanted a concrete plan. I made an appointment with the dietitian at the Cancer Center and had great expectations for the first meeting. It didn't work out quite as well. Martha was very nice, pretty knowledgeable, but clearly not moving as quickly as I. I left the first day with a transitional diet to vegetarianism, and I was past there.

My mom, having gone to the appointment with me, told me about Block Medical Center in Evanston, Illinois. She suggested calling them.

She said, "Evanston isn't that far away, we used to go for hockey with Josh quite often. If it's going to help it doesn't matter where it is. Just call and see what they say. Keith Block's name has come up in three books that I have read, I think it's worth checking it out." My mom, the researcher, strikes again.

A couple of days later I called. It was so easy. I explained my situation and that I would like to talk to someone about my diet. The woman on the phone asked me to send medical records, and bring what I couldn't send. They would set me up with a doctor, and then I would see the nutritionist. We made the appointment for my husband's birthday, February 15th.

Larry, my mom and my dad all went with me to Block. Driving down the night before we had dinner in a great Mexican restaurant a block behind the building. The day of my visit we all showed up and a nurse drew my blood. I hadn't been allowed to eat that morning because of the blood work and being accustomed to a large breakfast I was starved so after the draw we were shown into an unusual examining room and they brought me a snack. The room had an examining table, and the usual blood pressure equipment, but it also had a loveseat like you would find at home, big, soft, luxurious. Instead of providing paper gowns there was cloth and real throw blankets in which to cover up with. There was also a beautiful view of Evanston, the home of Northwestern University, all the way out to Lake Michigan.

After being in so many places in which to do tests or see doctors, this room was a beautiful respite. It was a place where you were a person, not just a patient. The comfort of the real blanket and cloth gown spoke of quality and care in this throw away world. Having real furniture rather than three vinyl covered chairs made the room inviting, a place to settle in and talk.

The snack threw me too. It was things they just had around, put on a plate for me. I felt as though I was eating someone's lunch. There was organic raisins, an organic apple juice box, a sort of windmill cookie, and nondairy butterscotch pudding. Of course I had gotten my green tea when we came in. The selection was put out instead of coffee. I knew that I was in for something different from my first visit with Martha.

Having already met the nurse we reviewed the past months of my life and she did the usual basic exam. Dr. Kut came in shortly after. She was not the picture that I have for a doctor exactly. She was beautiful, dressed very well, as though she could go out for the evening and fit right in. She had dark flowing hair that appeared styled rather than just combed quickly that morning. She didn't wear a lab coat, eliminating one barrier between doctor and patient.

Dr. Kut went through my history, asking questions about my current treatment and plans for the future. She questioned certain drugs, and generally provided contentment with the protocol. She explained that she would be happy to offer a second opinion in this situation, but that she also commonly directed chemotherapy and the like. I really liked her. I felt that she was honest and unobtrusive and yet very knowledgeable and clearly able to handle my treatment.

We laid out a plan to return in the summer, after my chemotherapy was over.

After Dr. Kut left I dressed and my family gathered in the room for the nutritionist. Where Dr. Kut was a slim person with a soft voice, David Grotto filled the room with his presence. He stood over six feet, and though not overweight there was a bigness about him, a gusto if you will.

"Heather, I'm Dave Grotto, so nice to meet you."

After introducing my family and exchanging pleasantries about the trip, we began to delve into nutrition. David provided a wealth of information, much of which was laid out in a three ring binder. He told us about Dr. Block, the founder of the center, and the research that he continually does so that what goes into our bodies is beneficial. Our bodies are amazing, having the ability to fight all sorts of disease, but it needs proper nutrients. The goal is to make the immune system as strong as possible, to get as much benefit as possible from the conventional treatment that I would be receiving, and to eliminate foods that feed cancer.

And then we began to talk about foods and eliminate a lot of what I ate in the past. Meat and dairy products were gone. My cancer was hormone-receptive and I did not need the hormones that come naturally or synthetically through shots that are given to animals for increased production. These products also have unnecessary antibiotic content and a lot of fat. When I asked about calcium, Dave told me of other great ways to get calcium. Hydrogenated and partially hydrogenated oils were next, followed by sugar and all of its family members.

I began to wonder what was left when David began to talk about what he would like to see me eat each day. Vegetables, 2 dark green leafy, 2 cruciferous, 2 root. Fruit, 1 citrus, 1 berry, 1 fibrous. Whole grains, brown rice, whole wheat breads, whole grain noodles, 15 servings a day. Protein, beans, some fish, soy products, 2 servings a day. By the time it was listed out, I knew it would be a challenge to eat it all. I asked Dave about my shake from Diana's book. He had just had her on the radio show that he hosts talking about her book and her plan. I was shocked to find that he knew her, and that he could put a stamp of approval on my shake with no trouble.

I left Evanston armed with a way to starve cancer and build a strong immune system. More importantly I left with validation that I could make a difference in this fight. I couldn't wait to get started.

Once home, I began my new way of eating, feeling confident that I was choosing what was best for me. I live in a small farming community, where vegetarians are for the most part nonexistent. However, God once again opened doors. Pam, my new friend, introduced me to the co-op she belonged to. I could order once a month and pick up my food at a local elementary school. Then the consignment shop in town closed, only to be replaced by Hometown Health Foods. I couldn't believe it. Even Helen's, the local restaurant, began to serve veggie burgers on whole-wheat buns and bottled water.

When you get to the edge of all the
light you know,
and are about to step off into the
darkness of the unknown,
Faith is knowing one of two things
will happen:
There will be something solid to
stand on,
or you will be taught how to fly.

-Barbara J. Winter

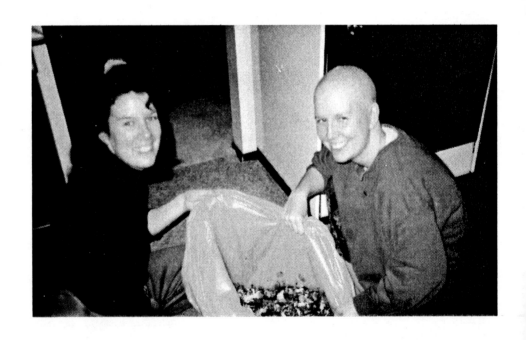

8. Preparing

Sydney Bs,

What is it that I really want you to know? Let's see: That I love you and I still can't believe that you are mine. That no matter what happens I am fighting as hard as I can to watch you grow up. That God has a plan in all of this. Some days I still can't believe that I really have cancer, although if I didn't we certainly would be going through a lot of unnecessary stuff. I still feel guilty for leaving you to work on me, but I'm praying it will be worth it. It's amazing how easily you adapt. Hair or no hair I'm still mommy. You're the best.

Love you,

Mommy

Sometimes things just go your way. When I was first diagnosed with cancer every single test that we did revealed more cancer, more problems, bleaker outcomes. It appeared though that we were beginning to see the light and move on to some better news.

Dear Friends,

Psalm 150:6 says, Let everything that has breath praise the Lord. We are praising, and singing, and high fiving everyday. We are killing cancer!! In the past five days my doctor has told me that she could no longer measure the 5-centimeter mass in my breast, and the bone marrow biopsy that we asked you to pray for came back clean, without cancer. My brain scan also came back clean a few weeks ago. God is hearing our prayers, and we again want to thank you for your faithfulness. Aside from the medical stuff I feel great. I have lots of energy, I've been working out most everyday, trying to eat 9-11 fruits and veggies everyday, drinking tons of water, taking vitamins, and spending quiet time with God each day. I've learned that I need to schedule healing time each day and our church friends have been very helpful in watching Sydney for me so that I can treat this like a job.

If you are a "what's next" person, this is the scoop. I finished my normal chemo. Next I'll begin stem cell collection so that they can freeze them and give them back later. This should take 2-4 days. My admit date is March 17. At that time I'll begin 96 hours of continuous chemo with the goal of killing all lurking cancer cells. I'll then get my stem cells back and they will stimulate them to grow. When my counts are high enough that I can fight some infection they'll let me out. The plan is that I would repeat another intensive chemo session in 6-8 weeks with another stem cell transplant at that time. Please pray that my insurance company approves this repeat procedure. They have done that in the past, but currently have denied it for me.

I have a job for anyone who reads this letter and keeps us in their thoughts and prayers. I know there are far more of you than I know so I am asking that you send me a picture of yourself and family if you are all involved. If you would like to send your favorite verse or quote I would appreciate that also. I have a healing notebook, which I want to fill with inspiration. The pictures will be a source of entertainment for me when I am in the hospital. Not because I expect them to be funny looking, rather because I plan on putting them in my photo album during my three week hospital stay. I'm a visual person and would really appreciate having a face connected with all the good thoughts that I've gotten from each of you. Peace to all.

Isn't it glorious! Isn't it grand!
Here-take it-hold it tight in your hand:
Squeeze every drop of it into your soul,
Drink of the joy of it, sun sweet and whole!
Laugh with the love of it, burst in to song!
Scatter its richness as you stride along!
Isn't it splendid- and isn't it great
We can always start living- it's never to late!
By Helen Lowrie Marshall
Heather

As the changes began to happen my spirits were really bolstered. During the meeting with Dr. Merajver after the brain scan came back normal she said nonchalantly, "I knew you were thinking all right."

As for the tumor being undetectable she told me, "We are clobbering the cancer!"

I loved her enthusiasm and her confidence. It energizes me to this day.

I was on my way to a stem cell transplant having made good on my statement to Dr. Ayash that my bone marrow biopsy would be clear. My doctors wanted to do another round of the usual tests to see where we were at. By this time I had an image for each one, to help everyone understand what they were like. There was the bone scan, which I called the tanner for the way it closed down on top of you; the CT scan, or the lifesaver because you passed through the middle of a round hole. And there was my least favorite, the MRI, which I deemed the thermos, the one you went into headfirst.

Around the time that I found out that I could do the transplants I was reading a book called, A Year of Miracles. It is about a woman who battled cancer in Ann Arbor and she really used a lot of meditative techniques, including making tapes specific for her in which to listen to with her treatment. Since I had had such good results with calling Block Medical Center out of the blue I called the doctor that she worked with too. We arranged to meet to be ready for the transplant. Together, in the course of three or four sessions, we were able to put together a meditative sequence specific to the drugs I was using.

The stem cell collection took two days. Of all the procedures I had done to this point, I liked this one the least, though it didn't hurt. In order to collect stem cells a large needle is inserted in the crux of each arm. The blood goes out through one needle and circulates through a machine that is able to collect stem cells and the blood goes back into your body through another needle in the other arm. The procedure takes about three hours to go through all the blood. During this time I was unable to move my arms at all. No itching my nose, no taking a drink, no changing the channel. Agony. I relied on my mom or Christy as I was stiff-armed, and they helped me through. They collected stem cells were frozen until later.

After finishing the stem cell collection the second day Christy and I went to Whole Foods to buy food were using to prepare meals for me while I was admitted. I knew I would have a tough time eating my diet while I was in so we wanted to bring in food instead. We bought tons of produce, much of which we had never tasted before to make a large salad. From the salad we would prepare other dishes, such as burritos which could be frozen.

After getting it back to Christy's parents house where she was staying we cleaned it all and began to mix it together. It got to be such a large quantity that no bowl was big enough to hold it all. We ended up shaking it up in a garbage bag.

In many ways it seemed as though we were back in high school that night. We were hanging out together, just having fun. Our neighbor Sam even came over for awhile. The radio was on, and the mood was light. At the end of the evening I called U of M and was ecstatic to find that they had enough stem cells and I didn't need to go back.

At home I was gathering things to take with me to the hospital. It was to be at least a three-week stay, so I was moving in. I put together a lot of pictures of Sydney and our family. I wanted everyone who came in to realize that I was a real person with a real life, not a bald, sick creature who only existed in the hospital. I made a large sign that said, "Every day we are killing cancer." I was serious about what I was there to do and I wanted everyone else to believe in me too. I brought all of my scrapbooking stuff, my CD and tape player for my meditation tapes and "Songs for Life" CDs, also a laptop computer to stay up on things. And I brought my quilt.

The healing quilt was the other thing that really impacted me in the *Year of Miracles* book. She had taken one with her each time to the hospital. I wanted to do the same. I am by no stretch a seamstress, but I had made a few quilts and so one day my mom and I picked out the fabric.

Christy and I were going to make it. We planned on doing it for a while, but when we finally got down to it we were under the gun, having started just two days before I was to be admitted. Chris came up on Sunday evening and we set up our sewing machines across the table from each other. Now Christy's mom makes incredible quilts, I had been the recipient of one for my high school graduation and one for my wedding. Christy, however, had no experience.

It was a great night. We sewed and sewed, ripped a few seams apart, and sewed some more. Late the next day we were finished, having spent a few hours crawling around on the floor to tie it. We had our moments of gigglyness, laughing at ourselves and the predicaments that we put ourselves in. The quilt looked amazing, vibrant colors, beautiful florals, and of course, U of M maize and blue.

I was ready to go.

Courage doesn't always roar.
Sometimes courage is the quiet voice
at the end of the day that says:
I will try again tomorrow.

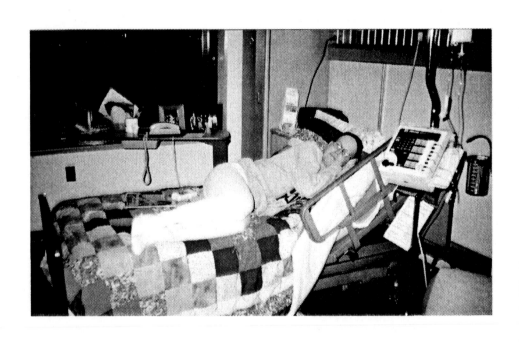

9. The Spa

Sydney Bs,

    I hate how different your life is from other little ones your age. Your parents talk about cancer, your mommy has to go away for a while. Will it affect you? Maybe make you stronger? I really don't know. I don't want you to be mad at God if I' not always here. I think it would just be part of the plan, though we don't know why. You are going to be a great girl. You've got your daddy's rhythm, picking up a beat just like nothing. I wonder if you'll be in the band. Or maybe play a sport. Who knows? I'll be thinking of you Syd.

I love you,

Mommy

My admit date came, March 17th. Though I'm not Irish, I was hoping to borrow a little of that luck. We had gathered together to pray before I came. It was a powerful time circled together in our living room. Sydney walked around and played as though nothing was happening, but it surely was, we were crying out to God.

It was a Wednesday morning. With the car packed full of stuff we went first to the cancer center. I couldn't believe I was stepping indoors for at least three weeks. I love being outside, even if just to walk to the mailbox. Before being admitted I needed to have a line placed. Up until this point whenever I needed to get something or they needed blood I would get an IV. The line was necessary for a few reasons: 1, I couldn't be able to handle the amount of needle sticks that I would need, 2 some of the drugs they were using were so powerful they wouldn't allow them to travel up my arm to enter my body, and 3 there would often be more than one type of fluid entering my body at any given time.

I was given the option early on to have a port of some kind placed so that a nurse or the vampires could easily access my veins. I chose not to do it as I didn't want something jutting out of my body to make me look different. I was already bald; my goal was to remain as human as possible in terms of equipment. It was a hang up of mine, but I felt very often that I was viewed as a disease, not a person, and the port seemed like one step closer.

The line placement was treated rather casually, as the doctor who performed does it all the time. I was able to do it right at the cancer center. It was later that it sunk in that the man had cut my jugular vein in order to put in the tube that came out of my body near my collarbone. The tubing had an end on it where three syringes or lines could go. It looked like the wiring on a car that you connect the trailer lights to. Anyway my jugular made it and because of that so did I. Now that I could be plugged in I was ready to go upstairs.

Christy and I had been calling my room at the hospital "the spa". It seemed so much more appealing to check into a spa to do some intense healing. In a real sense it wasn't appealing at all, but instead very sterile and uninviting. The University of Michigan Health System is immense, and just walking to my room on floor 8A from the cancer center involved a maze of hallways and elevators. After we found the correct wing I was shown to my room. The staff informed me that flowers had arrived for me before I had gotten there but since they were live I would not be able to enjoy them in my room. Already my show of support from friends had begun. After Larry made three very long trips to the car I had all of my stuff and was ready to settle in.

I filled the windowsill with all of the pictures

of my family and myself with hair. I had a view of the helicopter pad so I could watch it land and take off. I plugged in my CD player, and put away my tapes and CDs. On the bulletin board went the sign that read "Every day we are killing cancer" so that all could see it. I stashed my scrapbooking supplies, my puzzles and laptop and setup the card table that I had brought to work on. I left out the Magna Doodle and other small toys for Sydney to play with when she could visit. I filled the patient refrigerator with foods that I felt were good for me, as well as having a basket of dried fruits and other snacks in my room. Into my top drawer went my healing notebook and Bible. Finally I spread my quilt on my bed and color engulfed the sterileness. Be it ever so humble, it was nothing like home.

In came the nurses, raving over the quilt, getting ready to start the 96 hours of continuous chemo. I had the order of the drugs that would be used as I had used them to prepare my visualization. One nurse was very interested in the visualization, believing that it must help. I told her that I thought attitude was tremendously important.

And so it began, my time in the spa, with a nurse plugging in a line and letting the chemo flow while I listened to my tape and directed it to find any lurking cancer cells, believing that my body was meant to kill cancer and that God had plans for my future.

Larry went home in the evening beginning his time of juggling work, Sydney, and his wife in the hospital two and a half hours away.

That night before I went to sleep I called Christy, "You are gonna be here tomorrow right?"

"Yep. Want me to bring you a shake for breakfast?"

Ahh, good friends. Where would I be without her?

As the chemo flowed in I found myself feeling really good. I got to work on my scrapbook; I perused all of the take-out menus that were brought to me by Aunt Kathy. She told me just to place my order and someone would bring it up. She knew about my shake and her husband James, who is a chef, would make them for me in the mornings. I quickly put the dietitian on the defensive. She was not happy that she couldn't tell what I was eating as I wasn't consuming hospital food. She was very concerned that the shakes would have something in them that would infect me. She and I had differing opinions about nutrition.

On Friday night the chemo started to work, just like that it hit. It was Chinese night for dinner that night, and having just consumed some great fried rice I found myself feeling ill. I threw up all of it, and it would be the last thing that I ate for some time. As my counts began to drop I began to feel terrible. I had no energy, every thing that I put in my mouth I threw up. I

103

would feel like I could do something and then decide it would be better just to lie on my bed. The dietician's aide stopped asking me to fill out a menu and instead just smiled warmly and put it on my table.

Some mornings it was hard to stand for long enough to get a weight without getting dizzy. Though my job as an occupational therapist would have people getting up and getting ready by themselves in the hospital I thought the nurses were crazy when everyday they made me take a shower. The last thing on my mind was a shower. I was concentrating on standing, or sometimes just sitting without feeling woozy. They however seemed to have all the confidence in the world, leaving me to stand on my own in hot water, telling me if I needed to I could sit down.

Every morning Tracy, a PA, and others would round. She would check my counts and adjust medications. She would also play on the Magna Doodle that my mom had brought for Sydney. Tracy loved that thing. After a drawing a cat or some other doodling she would record my counts on a chart on my bulletin board.

I had a lot of visitors. Each day Larry, Christy, or my mom was there. A lot of days they all were. My room was where they met to pick up or deliver Sydney and to figure out how to get me something I wanted or needed. My mom did all of the dirty work, such as my laundry and special requests. It was she who would be there if others couldn't, or she would take Sydney so Larry could be with me. Larry's sister came up one night and we ordered pizza, Meredith's parents stopped in, as well as her brother and others in the Christian Medical Association. Even the Cooking Girls from my church ventured down and Pastor Jim was there a few times. The mail continued to pore in, eight or nine cards a day as well as emails racking up on my laptop.

Sydney was not a fan of my room. It was all too strange to her and she would hardly acknowledge me in that weird place. She preferred to ride the escalators. Though I understood, it was a bummer.

We watched my white blood counts decrease each day and bottom out at 7, normal is 4000-10000. With my counts bottomed out and the life of the chemo finished I was able to get my stem cells back. It was Wednesday March 24; I had been in one week. I was excited for the big day. Larry was planning on being there, but ended up with the flu so that he was having trouble even taking care of Syd. Christy drove up to our house to get Sydney and my mom came to the hospital to videotape the procedure which ended up being uneventful after all that I had built it up to be in my mind. Tracy came in with a small bag like the ones that get hung on an IV pole. It just looked like frozen blood. She put it in a bowl of water to unthaw the cells and then began to put them in my line using a large syringe. I began to cough a dry *hacky cough, which she had said would happen because of the preservative. Slowly she put them in and as she finished I threw up, also due to the preservative. That was it, a little cough, a little puke, and then life. Grow, grow, grow.*

I had thought I wasn't feeling well before the stem cells, and then I found out what not feeling well really felt like. My mouth began to get sore, actually more my throat, like a gigantic sore throat. The technical term was mucositis, and because of it I was started on a morphine drip. I continued to be unable to eat and I began to run fevers with unknown origins. During these days my visitors continued though I didn't always participate. Or sometimes I did join in, but I have no recollection of the conversations. A lot of time my mom, Larry or Christy were just there in case I would want to talk.

Christy's dad came up with her to see me one day. He was shocked at how easily Christy navigated her way through first the parking structure and then the maze of hallways and elevators in order to find me. Our lives had changed so much that she didn't even stop to think about being in this huge medical center.

I began to hate the aides who came in at 5:30 in the morning to take my vitals. Every morning they would make me get out of my nice warm bed and stand on the scale. It seemed as though if I needed help at night it took forever for someone to come, but when I finally really got to sleep in they came. It is true what they say about hospitals being a difficult place to sleep; it was quiet from about 11 at night until my early morning date with the scale.

I realized something in the middle of one of those nights. I realized that no matter how much help I had fighting cancer that ultimately it was just me and God. No one else would ever know what it felt like to do what I was doing. As much support as I had, in the middle of those dark nights it was just me and Him. It made me realize that the life that we live is only our own, and for the ultimate support God was the one on which to lean.

I did lean too. On one of those early mornings I found my chest feeling very heavy and breathing was not coming easily. My doctors ordered tests and found that I had developed pneumonia. I was scared, and almost angry. I had cancer, I thought that was enough; I didn't need all these other things. After all I had gone through I didn't want something like pneumonia to get the best of me.

Ten days after getting my stem cells they were up and growing. My morphine was discontinued and I began feeling better and pushing like crazy to get out. Dr. Ayash had the patience of a saint as I bugged her on rounds every day.

Throughout my stay Christy and I spent hours talking. I've come to believe that there are very few people in the world that you are comfortable enough to be with for hours on end, no matter what the situation. We had a lifetime of memories to draw on though, and passed time rather easily. She would do laps with me, pushing my pole or we would hang out in my room trying to figure out what was happening to our lives. The changes weren't all bad, but they were all encompassing and deep. Christy had jumped into things with both feet, trying everything I did. It was awesome. The day of my discharge we found ourselves having a discussion about how healthy we were. We were learning so much, that every day had so much to offer, that we spend far too much time on things that don't matter, that we had a say in how our lives went. And we were healthy, we were eating well, exercising, nurturing our spiritual lives. It was a crazy ironic thing to think that cancer brought life more abundant than we had ever known.

Armed with new knowledge, and awed by a God who brought me through the valley I was released 19 days after coming to the spa. It was the Monday after Easter, which had been my goal. We went to my mom's house to recover for a few days before heading North. Almost immediately I started feeling lousy. I was trying to eat but nothing tasted good, I even tried a glass of milk, which used to be a favorite. My taste buds were shot from all the chemo. I was guzzling Gatorade to keep from getting dehydrated. Try as I did I couldn't keep it together and one morning I passed out on the stairs. I woke up spewing Gatorade all over Larry and myself, something I'm sure neither of us will ever forget. I then tried to convince Larry that I would be just fine and there was no need to call anyone. He promptly called U of M and they told him to bring me in. He was right. I needed to go, but I didn't want to. I had just been freed two days earlier.

It was an interesting day in the Cancer Center. I was pretty dehydrated which is why I passed out so they hooked up an IV and got the fluids rolling. Dr. Ayash came in to see me. Again I'm begging her, this time that I won't be admitted back to 8A. She cranked up the saline drip and made me a deal. If I could stand up for two minutes without any trouble by the time the Cancer Center closed at 9:00pm I could go home, if not, welcome back 8A. I told her that I felt great; I was even eating chicken nuggets and a potato from Wendy's. She smiled and said she couldn't believe I was eating that stuff, meaning most people go for bland, not fried nuggets. I knew it wasn't a great nutritional choice, but hey, it was working for me.

The challenge was on, all afternoon and evening I would think I could do it so I would call in Chrissy, an aide, and have her time me. Each time I failed, but it was funny, me getting all geared up just to stand for two minutes. Another example of one of those things you would never think would be humorous and than you learn about cancer humor. So back I went, with all the nurses up on the floor telling me they knew I wasn't ready to leave on Monday.

I spent two nights there, eating popsicles, watching 101 Dalmatians in the middle of the night, and talking to docs. Two doctors rounded on Saturday and I watched my dream of going home fade in a cruel way. Dr. Uberti was with Dr. Reynolds, Dr. U being the senior doctor asked Dr. Reynolds if after reviewing my chart he thought it was okay for me to go home. Dr. Reynolds, being cautious, told me he would like me to stay one more night. Dr. Uberti said that was fine, though he probably would have let me go. Just what I wanted to hear. Ugh.

After another long night Sunday morning came and I was sitting outside my door waiting for Dr. Ayash to round. It was barely 7:00 am. When she saw me waiting in the hall she told me she would come and see me first. She came in and brought a resident with her. While doing my exam she tells the resident that I have made remarkable progress, and that she is very pleased. She couldn't have paid me a higher compliment; Dr. Ayash's words are few and meaningful. To top it off she let me go home.

That which does not kill us
makes us stronger.

-Anonymous

10. Round Two

Sydney Bs,

  My favorite time of year is the spring. I love seeing things growing everyday, the leaves coming out on the trees, the tulips and daffodils pushing through the ground for another year. My favorite color is red. I love its vibrancy, and it's strength. My favorite ice cream flavor is mint chocolate chip, though I shouldn't have it anymore. My favorite car is a Fiat. I almost talked my dad into getting me one. My favorite job was working as a camp counselor, I loved having fun everyday, being crazy, singing before every meal. It was the greatest. My favorite wish is that I will know all of your favorites. My favorite girl is you.

Mommy

Ahh, freedom. I was so glad to be home, but I was far from ready to be on my own. We went back to our home, my mom coming along to help out for a few days. I was no longer feeling any nausea, but I wasn't ready to resume my normal routine either. We walked in to a clean house, courtesy of the cooking girls from church, and our dog had been given a complete check up and bath courtesy of Karen, Pastor Jim's wife. It took some time to unpack as I had accumulated so many things while in the hospital, and Sydney added to her growing collection of toys.

Figuring out our days took a little planning. I wasn't suppose to change messy diapers, due to the possibility of germs and though I could take care of myself, Sydney was a little out of my league energy wise. We had many offers of baby-sitting for Syd, but I didn't want her to be gone, I hadn't seen her in some time. And so, Christy came up and stayed, people from church came through again and we made it through the first weeks back at home. It led to me feeling helpless, sitting on the couch while others vacuumed, made me lunch and took care of my child. I was the scheduler, that was it. What a humbling time.

Everyday I got stronger though, and soon it was time to write another letter.

Dear Friends,

Hebrews 10:35 says, So do not throw away your confidence; it will be richly rewarded. I haven't thrown it away, but I must say it has faltered. I'm not sure if that is because I spent so much time away from the places that give me strength or because U of M makes cancer their problem and not Gods. In any case now that I am home I'm searching for the strength and confidence that was once mine, I'm sure that I can find it again.

It is wonderful to be home, to go to baseball games and church, to play outside with Sydney. I thank God that I only had to spend three weeks in the hospital; some on my floor were doing 3-month stints. It was also wonderful to be the one with the most mail everyday, with prayers being said for me when I was working on just existing, and with any food being brought up to me every day that I was eating. Thank you all for your help in my healing; this truly is a group effort.

I know you have medical questions and to be honest so do I. My second transplant was approved by my insurance company and will likely be coming up in 3-4 weeks. I begin doing tests again this week. The second transplant is an outpatient procedure if I can stay away from infection. I will be staying at my parents house and going to Ann Arbor everyday. I will be doing a different set of chemo drugs on a different schedule than before. I do not know what happens after the transplant. Surgery is a possibility as is radiation. I have not had any feedback lately as to the cancer being gone or not; however two of my youngest prayer warriors have stopped praying about the cancer, not concerned about it anymore.

In the answered prayers column we continue to add many things. After being told that I had pneumonia in the hospital I was given a chest x-ray two days after getting out and it was completely gone. They said it wasn't the same girl. God works swiftly sometimes. I also continue to get letters on a regular basis that start out you don't know me but... These are the best, feeling as though cancer is making people's faith stronger and encouraging us all the reach out and embrace each other.

For prayer concerns I would ask that you continue to pray for healing, negative test results, and that I would be directed to use this cancer and my life to change other lives. I'm not sure how, but I may have some interesting possibilities. I would also encourage you to pick a few other people who weigh on your heart to talk to God about. Thank you for all the pictures, my book didn't get very far in the hospital, as I was too busy throwing up. If you would still like to send pictures, I have plenty of space to put them in. For those of you who would like a picture of me (bald or with hair), I'd be happy to send you one, just let me know. I'll continue to keep up my end of the correspondence and would love for you to keep yours, either through mail or email (which is addictive and very simple for those of you not online). Happy spring. Hope you enjoy every sunny day. Have a great day.

Love,

Heather and Larry

With the testing going well, we made plans for the second transplant. This one would be outpatient, meaning I would go to the infusion center everyday, but I could go home after getting whatever was scheduled. Most patients ended up being admitted, however, due to infection or severe mouth pain. My goal was to stay out the whole time. I resumed walking and eating well, as well as taking my supplements and nurturing my soul. As my strength returned so did my determination, I was ready to begin.

It started on a Monday this time, May 10th. I went to the cancer center to have a line placed again, as my other one was removed before I left the spa on my previous visit. I wasn't nervous this time, and found myself joking with the nurse as she got me ready. Little did I know it was training day, and I was the guinea pig. Actually, there was a doctor in the room to learn the procedure, and so the doctor performing the placement was narrating exactly what was happening. It wasn't a big deal at first, but as he was placing the line in my vein it didn't just go in smoothly as before. Maybe because it had been done once and there was some scarring, maybe it just wasn't a good day. Anyway, as he is talking to the doc I am hearing everything that is being said, and it made it more painful. I know that is probably all in my head, but it just shows how powerful our thoughts can be, for good or for bad.

Once punctured and ready to receive fluids I went to the infusion room where they hooked me up to my chemo, Taxol this time, which was then put in to a fanny pack. It was to run for 24 hours, and I would be back the next day for the next procedure. I set the time for my return and off we went. Seeing as it was Christy accompanying me that day we chose to go to out to lunch and to our favorite natural foods grocery store, no reason to waste a good day together. It was the weirdest thing, shopping while getting chemo, one thing so lighthearted, one thing so serious. Once at our parents' houses we went out on the boat. We felt compelled to live and enjoy every day. So though bald, and hooked up, we had fun.

Our daily treks to Ann Arbor had begun, the first day for chemo, the second to remove my fanny pack and get fluids, the third day more chemo, this time at the center. On Thursday I got my stem cells back, this time without any trouble, and with Larry there to see it.

My brother Troy came home from Texas and he came with me one day. He checked out everything and took off to find some old friends in the hospital. God love him, by the time he returned I was already done and ready to go. So much for hanging out. He did a great job of managing all my medication though, as I was taking multiple pills for nausea, heartburn, pain, and others. He made a chart that we all followed to get them all in on time.

Two days after getting my stem cells back I was

still feeling good, moving around the house, playing with Syd. I was drinking a ton as my throat was getting dry, and I didn't want to get dehydrated. By Sunday I was throwing up on the way to Ann Arbor and home, and I was sure I'd be getting admitted. My throat kept getting thicker.

As I began to feel worse I spent my time at my parents' house laying on the futon, watching Disney videos with Sydney. There was one Pongo and Perdia video that was played again and again. It brings on feelings of being sick all by itself. But it was good to be home.

God Bless my drivers, Larry, my mom, or Christy usually. After the transplant I would still go everyday to get fluids and one day I got a blood transfusion. The difference in the way I felt was immediate, more energy, a little spring in your step, it was incredible. Since then, I am all for transfusions, and grateful to the many who donate their blood. My doctors did a great job of managing my pain and other problems, because of them I struggled through and made it through the whole thing without spending the night. On the second Saturday I was given the okay to not come back until Tuesday, and then they would remove my line. I was the second of 10 patients to make it through without going in. It was an accomplishment that made me proud.

People are like stained glass windows

They sparkle and shine when the sun

is out

But when darkness sets in,

Their true beauty is revealed only

If there is light from within.

-Elizabeth Kubler-Ross

11. The New Me

Sydney Bs,

     Here is my advice on dating. 1. You can't fool Daddy and I; don't even try. 2. Be too busy sometimes; a little chase is good for everyone. 3. Be yourself; after all that is who you will always be. 4. Don't settle for okay; find the one who makes your heart sing. 5. When you are happy with who you are it shows, and people are attracted to you. 6. Dream big. 7. Know that no one, even Prince Charming, will be good enough in your daddy's eyes. What an amazing thought to think that someday you'll be all grown up.

I love you,

Mommy

We spent a sunny Fourth of July with our friends out on their boat. It was a great day of relaxing and hanging out, with a minimal amount of cancer talk. I went into surgery with a good attitude.

Dr. Pass, my surgeon, was really nice. A mother of four-year-old twins, this was a lady who carried on as your friend, not the director of the breast care clinic at a major university hospital. She was easy to talk to and understood my fears and concerns. I was amazed and thankful that again I found a great doctor.

My surgery was scheduled for the morning and so after saying good-bye to Sydney and leaving her with Larry's parents we set off for the U once again. Today we were going to a part of the hospital that was new to me, another place to find our way around. After parking and walking in to the main hospital entrance we found a large room for the people waiting to have surgery. I checked in and was told to have a seat. It was fairly full in the room but we found a spot to wait for my turn. I looked about and found myself wondering what all these people were here for. I had never thought of surgery as a planned event as much as something that you might be rushed in for unexpectedly. By the look of this place however it seemed as though a lot of people planned ahead.

Time past and we waited. My scheduled time came and went and after a while Dr. Pass came in to see me. She was running behind, but not worried. She said I would be in that afternoon. I was glad for a chance to talk with her; I wanted to be sure that she knew about my choice to have a double mastectomy. With that all cleared up I felt at ease and we spent the afternoon playing cards, Larry and my parents, as if we were just hanging out at home. I was finally called in at four to get ready for the next step.

When I was first diagnosed with the cancer my initial reaction was that I wanted in out, now. I was surprised to find that the surgery would come later. But as I went through the chemo and could actually see the changes in my breast as the tumor shrank it was incredibly reassuring. If I had had surgery first I wouldn't have seen the progress that I had already made to this point. I wasn't emotionally wrought over losing a part of my body; in fact I tried to see it in a positive light, such as no more bras. I guess more than anything I felt that losing my breasts were a small price to pay for life.

My surgery went smoothly and though I didn't get into the operating room until 5:45 I was done by 8:30. They had estimated four to six hours, but hadn't needed all the time. Tissue and lymph nodes were sent to be biopsied so we would know if there were any cancer cells there.

I spent the night and called Christy early the

next morning asking for a shake. She was happy to oblige my request and to hear that I was feeling like eating. When she came up I asked her if she wanted to see my chest. I was amazed at the way it looked, because it almost seemed normal to me. Just a flat chest, nothing more, nothing less. The gross part was these ugly drains that I had for the excess fluid. I had all of my lymph nodes removed on the left side so I had two drains on that side, on the other I had just one. They repulsed me, after everything I had been through, blood and vomit I was grossed out by the drains and I wanted them out.

Feeling good, though sore, I was released that afternoon, less than 24 hours after going in to the OR. I went back to my parents for a few days to recover and have help with Sydney. Two days later I had two of the drains taken out and six days after surgery the final one was removed. I was pleased with my progress and so we headed back home and I continued to work on moving my arms.

The tough part about the surgery was Sydney. As glad as I was that she didn't understand most of my treatment I would've given anything for her to understand why I couldn't pick her up. A 10 pound weight limit and a 20 pound daughter just don't agree. It broke my heart as we taught her to climb up the step stool and in to her crib. I could then put the rail up and she could sleep as always. I would cajole and beg her to walk with me *instead of being carried. I felt as though the cancer was now affecting her, and that made me mad. Hurting me was one thing, but leave her alone. She wanted to climb on me, to snuggle close, but it was too painful. We were able to put a pillow between her and I so I could read to her, in order to pacify us both.*

In no time at all I was back to walking and as active as always, with the exception of the weight limitations. It was time to tackle the last phase.

You have to climb the mountain

to appreciate the view.

-Grace Easley

12. Radiation Woes

Sydney Bs,

I always knew there was a God. I just never thought about how interested He was in me. You know I've been praying a lot lately and I can feel Him closer to me. I feel as though He is helping me find the way and He is providing the people that we need to be okay. Imagine that. God wants to talk with me. I bet that in your life you'll have times of feeling close or far from God but I pray that you'll always know that He loves you, so much that He let His own son die for you. Sometimes it seems hard to hear God, but many times I think we just don't listen. I think He speaks through people and things that happen in our lives if we notice these things. The question is "if". I love you Silly.

Mommy

The preparation for radiation began. I had done my part, I could keep my arm above my head and so I was ready to get started. But first I had to make a decision about my job. My medical leave had only been granted through the end of the school year, and now I had to look at whether or not I could go back in the fall and maintain the things that I felt were crucial to staying healthy. I chose, with my husband's support, to resign. Radiation would be going in to the beginning of the school year by about a month anyway and I wasn't ready to try to juggle it all.

We began to map out radiation. The doctor that I met in Ann Arbor, Dr. Lori Pierce, was great. She had received many awards in her profession but mostly she was just nice, and confident and charging forward. All the things I liked in a doc. However, after meeting with her we agreed that it would be better for me to receive the radiation in Lansing, saving me two hours a day of driving time. U of M had a partnership with a radiology department there and so Dr. Pierce could oversee the treatment, though I would be working with a doctor in Lansing as well.

I pushed to get things going quickly as July was fading fast and August in our house means two things: football season and good bye Larry.

We began in Lansing by meeting my newest doctor, yet another woman, and having more tests done. The plan was to do radiation to the left chest region and lymph nodes as reoccurrence tend to be at the original breast cancer site. My tissue samples from the surgery had come back great, with no sign of cancer cells. So the radiation was just another punch to keep the cancer from returning. I wanted them also to radiate a spot on my spine where I tended to have some pain. It wasn't overly painful, but it would freak me out, thinking that the cancer was back. I wasn't successful however; they weren't going to touch my spine. My lung would be in the way though, and would lose about 10 percent of its function. I was told I would not even notice, as I could live with just one lung if needed. I would be going five days a week for six weeks.

After the testing and talking I met with the radiation techs who would make a mold of my body so that I could lay on a form that would position me in the exact same spot each day. They started out by having me lay on a table with my shirt off and began to draw all over my chest with permanent marker. The comments were that they were just doing a little art and could I please not shower so that they could see their masterpiece the next day. I had had enough. Here I was, basically bald, with no chest and people were joking around as they drew all over me. I felt like I wasn't even a person to them, just another part of their day. I was truly fed up with being called a CAT scan (or whatever test I was having),

having things minimized and made light of, and generally being dehumanized in the eyes of the technicians of the medical community. When they told me that they would be placing permanent tattoos on me for landmarks I about flipped. I wanted to know why they needed them, how big they would be and how many they would place. After some serious negotiations we agreed to two small dots, one on my upper chest and one below my armpit. Neither would be bigger than the tip of a sharpened pencil.

That day I vowed, if I ever returned to work in a hospital setting, that I would try to know patients as individuals, to understand some background or something beyond the diagnosis that accompanied their name. I would try to keep in mind that they are likely part of a family that loves them and doesn't see them only in a medical light. And I would not make light of their situation for my benefit. Some day I would love to teach a class on how not to belittle patients to all the techs I encountered.

Dear Friends,

Are you ready for some football? The high school season starts tomorrow. So do my radiation treatments. After being put off a lot longer that I thought we are ready to go. I'm actually looking forward to a routine; I'm so much more productive.

My surgery went well on July 6, and I'm healing everyday. I notice fewer arm movements all the time. My range of motion is close to full and definitely functional. (I know all my OT and PT buddies need to know that.) The coolest thing is that there was no living cancer in any tissue or lymph nodes. If you ever wondered whether or not miracles still exist you can be sure they do, and that is one. I really wasn't slowed much by the surgery, I went putt putting 5 days later, and carried on as usual with the exception of lifting. Sydney has been climbing into her crib with the help of a stool and seems to enjoy that.

I will not be going back to work in the fall as an occupational therapist. This was a difficult decision for me as I've always seen myself working and I had a great job. I will not be done with my radiation before school starts though and I still need a significant amount of time each day to dedicate to healing. I have gotten involved with our church youth group and plan to become more active. I continue to ponder God's plan for me and what I should be doing each day. I want to make a difference everyday. Any suggestions will be considered. Sydney B will be going to daycare most days to allow me healing time. We are fortunate to be blessed with great people to watch her and she just started in a real daycare setting, which she loves.

The metropolis of Remus is helping me eat healthy. A health food store just opened, and will meet my needs in terms of groceries. Helen's, the local restaurant, is also carrying gardenburgers on whole-wheat buns and bottled water. Way to go!! If you are a local receiving this letter please support these places, it helps me tremendously.

I haven't much more to say, we continue to look forward to upcoming events and to know with it is we are here to do. I was looking for a devotion time to do with the youth the other day and I came across this, a favorite from my college days. Wouldn't it be great if we really looked at life this way?

God Bless,

Heather

To laugh often and love much;

To win the respect of intelligent people and the affection of children;

To earn the appreciation of honest critics and endure the betrayal of false friends;

To appreciate beauty;

To find the best in others;

To leave the world a bit better, whether by a healthy child, a garden patch,

or a redeemed social condition;

To know even one life has breathed easier because you have lived;

This is to have succeeded.

Ralph Waldo Emerson

Radiation was a massive coordination nightmare. I had arranged for someone to watch Sydney every morning. Then the scheduler at radiology told me that I would have to come in the afternoon as mornings were too busy with other patients. I told her no, that she would need to put me in; I couldn't rearrange my drivers and daycare that was already established. I was putting my foot down; I was not in the mood to negotiate. I just wanted it done. It got done.

Radiation has a tendency to make people tired so I tried to have drivers as many days as possible. I made a little calendar and passed it around at church. Those sitting the closest to us in the pews all got a chance to take an exciting trip to Lansing; estimated time of trip 4 hours. I had a pretty good response and of course Christy filled in as well.

So it began, I would get up, take Sydney to daycare and come back to go to Lansing. While there I would wait in the patient waiting room which always had a puzzle on the table to work. A great idea, I must say, as it passed the time quickly and if they were running behind I never cared. The radiation itself took about two minutes once I was positioned on my form and they left the room.

I would lay still and the machine would rotate to three different angles that being used. Buzz, buzz, buzz, see you tomorrow.

I ran into a stumbling block the end of my first week of radiation. I was having some itching in my hairline (what little there was of it). It felt like a tiny pimple that wouldn't pop. On Friday I saw the doctor after my treatment who told me it was shingles. I had no idea what that was. The doc called U of M and they wanted me to be sent me to Ann Arbor for further evaluation. Shingles is a form of the chicken pox virus and very common after a transplant. With radiation putting more stress on my immune system it broke out. The problem was that it was on the left upper quadrant of my head, possibly in my eye, where it could cause blindness.

Darn, there I am at U of M on a Friday afternoon and what happens? I got admitted for the weekend so that I could be on IV antibiotics. Of course, had I gotten there earlier the doctor who puts in pic lines (a special type of IV) would have been there and I could have had the drugs at home with visiting nurses. But no such luck, and welcome back.

After an uneventful stay I was released on Monday, ready to start back with the radiation.

The folks in Lansing said that I was contagious and therefore the morning appointments that I fought so hard for would not be possible as I could expose someone else. Instead I was to come in the late afternoon. Since I was on medication I was no longer contagious, but they didn't care. It completely ruined my daycare situation and made me all the more unhappy with the whole situation.

When I was able to return to my morning spot a week or so later the gentleman that I always chatted with asked where I had been and I found out that he had been dealing with shingles on his stomach since before *my outbreak. Since the spots were covered they didn't make him change his time, and he probably exposed me to begin with. I continued to lose respect for this establishment.*

In many ways though I was doing really well. Every week I would meet with the doctor who told me that I would have second to third degrees burns in the chest area. She didn't know that I had called Block and they had suggested changes to my diet and a few special supplements to get through this time. I barely even turned pink. After one appointment the doctor offered me a piece of candy from the candy dish on the counter.

I looked at her and said, "No thanks, sugar feeds cancer". All she could do was shake her head; I was way too intense for her.

I began having a little trouble with lightheadedness in the morning. Glenna, one of the cooking girls from church, a true Texas princess begrudgingly living in the north, came to pick me up for my date in Lansing. She opened the door to find me lying on the floor by the door. Freaking out, she asked what I needed her to do, call an ambulance, anything. I told her that if she would get me a glass of orange juice I'd be ready in a minute. Just a glass of juice? Glenna was ready to hook me up to a machine. Once I had drunk the juice, I was upright and ready to go, though she wasn't the same. Learning from my experience I began to have Larry put a glass of OJ on the nightstand for me to drink before I tried to move around. It worked fine.

As we approached the end of radiation Larry and I saw an ad on TV about Race for the Cure, a 5K event to raise money for breast cancer sponsored by the Komen Foundation. We decided to walk it, and I set a goal to run it the following year. I sent out a letter asking for pledges and we went to the race early one Saturday in September. It was a first for me to be honored as a survivor, and I had mixed feelings of pride and humbleness, as well as joy and sadness that we had found ourselves there. But the event was awesome, the walk itself interesting with many people cheering us on. Poor Larry ended up carrying Sydney almost the whole way as she refused to sit in her stroller, but we finished with smiles and a good feeling in our heart.

I finished radiation on a Tuesday, jumping for joy that I was done. Besides the shingles, which had screwed up the nerves in my forehead, I was no worse that when I started. I and still didn't have that burn that my doc told me would be there.

Courage is fear that has said it's

prayers.

-Author Unknown

13. On My Shoulders

Sydney Bs,

What do you do when you are scared? I always talk to Daddy. He's so good at putting things in perspective. Being scared is okay sometimes. It motivates us to do things that we might not if everything were okay. It teaches us that we all need each other. I've been scared a lot lately. I'm wondering if the cancer is really gone, if I can move forward in my life. I don't know if I'll be okay without doing some kind of treatment. I don't know who I am anymore. Oh that's right, Sydney's mom. I'll start with that. Thank God for you.

Love,

Mommy

My final treatment ended ten months after my diagnosis of breast cancer. Cancer had taken my world and turned it upside down. It had shown me the mountains and the valleys and now I was supposed to start living a normal life again. As usual with the completion of treatment I wrote a letter to my friends.

To My Faithful Followers,

Ahhhhh, it's over, I'm done, finished, complete. I think I have done every treatment they could think of for killing breast cancer. I'm grateful for all of the treatments, as they all have their place in my journey. It just became a long road at the end. Radiation was a pain. Too much driving and planning drivers and no time working out and spending quiet time with God. It was also the first encounter with a doctor who lacked confidence in me and was easily intimidated by my questions. So after that pleasant experience I'm ready to move on.

It's beautiful outside. The fall colors are brilliant. Our house faces an asparagus field that is a bright yellow with a tree line behind showing all sorts of reds, yellows and greens. With the changing of the trees my focus will also change. I'm going to learn how to meditate. Survivors generally rank this as the most important change in their lives after cancer. I'm going to make my body strong physically. I set up a program with a trainer today at a wellness center near my home. I'm going to eat well everyday. I will be starting on a detox program to rid my body of residual chemicals and toxins which make functioning more difficult.

I will spend quiet time every day with God, and I will journal my thoughts. Aside from that I will try to be a good mom to my great daughter, a good football wife to my husband, and a dedicated youth leader to an exceptional youth group. I feel as though there is a lot on my plate, but it is all positive. Who could ask for more?

Many of you haven't heard from me in some time, my surgery went well, I already spoke of radiation, and my fun experience with shingles continues. Fortunately, it is being controlled quite well with medication, but I'm careful not to miss a dose. My body is doing a better job of fighting off illness on its own, which is nice. I don't have to be back in Ann Arbor until the end of November, Praise God!! At that time a complete check will be done, and hopefully a report of no cancer once again. These checks will occur at least twice a year.

You also may not know that Larry and I walked in Grand Rapids' Race for the Cure. It was a great experience. I raised $1100.00 in five day's time. Thank you for the fast and very generous contributions. All the money goes to the Komen Breast Cancer Foundation. I hope to run it next year, and to win the individual prize, which was won at $3600.00 this year. I'll start earlier, give you a little more notice.

So, now it's me and God, and we're gonna hold off this monster that we call cancer. I'm going to see my baby go to kindergarten; I want the opportunity to adopt another child someday. We have hearts full of love; we're hoping that God shows us the children that need it the most. Psalm 53:6 says When I'm afraid, I will trust in

149

you. That is what this is about now, trusting and having confidence that it can be done. I thank you all for your tremendous support; I know it will continue through your prayers. We've learned a lot about life, and how precious it is, I hope that you have too. I'm not sure I'm qualified to give advice but I'd challenge each of you to make your own life better everyday, in little ways. They sure make a difference. I'll be sending a Christmas card; you won't believe all the hair on my head. I hope to hear from you too.

God be with you,

Heather

From there I began to slowly build a new life. One devoted to wellness, to family, to awareness of the world around me. Some days I was on top of the world, feeling sure that the miracle was complete and I was healed of cancer. Other days I felt sure that the pain in my back was certainly cancer and I dove into my healing notebook for support as I prayed.

It was hard for me to find worth in what I was doing. If someone were to ask what I was doing now that my treatment was over I didn't think that trying to stay healthy was an acceptable answer. I found out first hand how little being a stay at home mom meant to society. I'm not sure why it was such a struggle for me to define myself or why the need to do so was so strong.

One day I found myself scribbling frantically on the back of a piece of paper:

At one point my life was crashing down around me and everything was hard, now the tide is out and life does not crash. But that glorious view is gone. It is easy to become lackadaisical, not on guard anymore; the voice of God is not as clear, nor as intense. Jesus, it is difficult for me to not be among the crashing surf, though it is tiring to be in it. I pray that my rest can be to nurture myself and to be prepared to be strong enough to enter the surf again. It need not be the same as before, nor must it be directed by me, I pray though that I will be there again, engulfed in the intensity and power of life and God as the control. Lord help me to use my low tide to walk with others along the journey that has been given to each of us. Please engulf me in the spirit again.

I was shocked reading it later at how well that brief writing described the battle within myself.

Step by step I moved forward, establishing a routine of going to the wellness center, continuing to work on eating well, getting involved in church. Some days Sydney and I would go up to the high school to visit Larry because I needed to be around adults, even if I wasn't actually working there.

Since I was now deemed healthy once again people expected that I would be returning to normal again. I wasn't able to do that. Too much had happened, too many things changed. The constant complaints about little things that I would hear drove me crazy. I found myself wanting to tell everyone that they should be focusing on all the good things.

Christy and I continued to be in constant communication and more and more it was her that was having a tough time. She left her husband and was trying to work through many things in her life, including the guilt for not being able to fix her marriage. She was spending time at her grandmother's house, which was less than an hour away so we would try to get together whenever we could. Although armed with the knowledge that each day was precious we were also acutely aware of the battles we had fought learning our new perspective.

Live pure, speak true, right wrong,

Follow Christ, the King.

-Lord Tennyson

14. Blessings

Sydney Bs,

You are my sunshine, my only sunshine, you make me happy when skies are gray... What a beautiful girl you are. We have survived the battle, now if we can just keep on surviving. You are growing so fast, becoming a little girl, cooing to your babies, cooking with the girls. One day you'll be all grown up. I will always love you. I will always be proud of you. I will always be amazed that God blessed me with you. Reach for the stars Sydney B, follow God and make your mark on this old world.

Hugs,

Mommy

I ended the year with a final letter to the masses.

Dear Friends,

11 shopping days until Christmas. I mean Merry Christmas! I hope all is well in your house, and that you are enjoying the season for what it is, a time to enjoy family and focus on the birth of Christ. I probably wouldn't have been so bold as to say that last year. Isn't it strange how God teaches us what is really important.

We are truly enjoying Christmas festivities right now. Sydney is at a great age to think everything from lights to presents is the best thing ever. She is talking up a storm, surprising us with words everyday. She was an angel in the Christmas program at church, and did quite well. Larry is keeping busy at school teaching and opening the weight room for his football players. We are looking forward to going to Florida for the week before Christmas. (I know Mom, I'm not suppose to tell the world like Dad always does.) There is nothing like that dose of sunshine in December. I don't care what all you "snow for Christmas" people think.

Do you want a medical update? I went back to Ann Arbor right before Thanksgiving, and the tests that they had looked fine. That means that there are no tumors according to a CAT scan of my chest abdomen and pelvis. I still have to do a bone scan, scheduled for 12/27 so please pray for a clear scan there too. I'm anxious to have one totally clear scan under my belt. Other than that I feel great. I'm not tired, I'm not weak, I'm stronger than ever. Please believe that. I've had fewer colds than Larry and Sydney this fall. My doctor told me I have abs of steel; it's always nice to hear that. Crunches work, I guess. I got my first haircut a few weeks ago. Some things I am unwilling to change, so I drove back to Jackson to have the person that I wanted trim my new locks.

Last year at this time I had just been diagnosed. What a yucky, scary time. It all seems like a black cloud settled on that part of my memory. I can't think of a lot of bright spots. My first letter to you was also written about this time last year. Since then the changes in my life have been enormous, and worthwhile. I'm not sure I could express the ways in which I have changed. Nor do I know if you could ever relate, unless touched by a situation yourself. I don't want my life to go back to the way it was before cancer because then what would I have learned? God sent me on this journey for a reason. For me it seems more important to just drink it in and be conscious of every swallow. There are many positives to be found in a negative situation, and I feel this is how I can use this situation to God's glory. I feel rather preachy at times, wanting people to acknowledge the goodness that is in their life.

With that I will leave you. Have a Merry Christmas and a Happy New Year. You can't imagine how ready I am to move on to a new millennium. May the Y2K bugs be uneventful.

Peace On Earth,

Heather

It seems to me that there is a cancer in everyone's life, though it does not always come with a, 'you have six months to live' attached. The crazy thing is that out of those cancers come the sweetest most meaningful moments in our lives. The kind words of a stranger, the embrace of your spouse, the laughter of a child all make memories that will never be forgotten. On our wedding day the minister's final prayer for us was that God would give us enough challenges to keep us walking with Him. Although there were many times when I thought back on that with mixed feelings, I've learned to thank God for the challenges.

It has been a crazy thing for me to deal with the reality that I am here in spite of dismal odds. My cancer was advanced to the point of it being terminal. That I have the opportunity to parent my child and be a wife is a miracle, plain and simple. I do not know why God chose me. Sometimes I wonder if it were not for the many people praying for me would I even be here.

The thought of having cancer will always remain in my mind. I find myself surprised if I've made through a whole day without thinking of it. The reminders are everywhere. I can fight cancer again if I need to, though I pray that doesn't become necessary. I would rather that the thought of cancer remind me to make use of the day that I have been given. This is not what I had envisioned for my life, but in many ways it is better.

It has made me dig within myself to look for what God may have planned for me rather than what I planned for myself. I know that I am living on God's time, but when thinking about that I realized that we all are.

May God bless you with a challenge, and may you feel the outpouring of love that I have. Reach out; someone is waiting to embrace you.

Afterword

I now have had many good reports of no progression of cancer. What a blessing. There have been many others. I reached my 30*th* birthday, a benchmark for me. I celebrated by walking the Avon Breast Cancer 3 Day with Christy and Katie. We walked twenty miles a day for three days and raised over $7,500.00. We were cheered on along the way by Larry and Sydney. Also encouraging us were Christy's mom as well as my grandparents, my parents, and my in-laws. It was awesome. Larry and I were blessed with a son, Ty Dustin, born in India and placed in our family with God's faithful help. He is a gift, and if it took cancer to find him it was all worth it. The adoption process is another book in itself, but let me just thank Sharin for being so persistent. I also reached the goal of watching my daughter go to kindergarten, bawling as she rode away on the bus to begin her first day in Chris Cotton's class.

Acknowledgements

I would not be here writing without the faithful prayers of many. Some of these I will never even know, but I must mention a few by name. To my New Hope church family, and especially Mike and Beth, bless you. God is good, all the time. For those of you who jumped on board and truly believed I am eternally grateful. To Matt, Lyle, and my mom who continued to ask about my book, thank you for the loving encouragement. Thank you Grandma Ahlstrom, a prayer warrior in every sense who daily brings me before God.

To my awesome medical team, which is more extensive than even those mentioned in this book. Thank you for your spirit, drive, and care that is saving lives. May you all continue to clobber cancer for many years to come.

Christy, what an awesome friend you are. I am so glad that God made us neighbors so that we could be friends. May we have many more adventures together. Thanks for standing with me, it makes life so much better.

To Larry, you rock! Without you I would miss out on so much love and laughter. Thank you for being my friend, my coach, and for believing in the miracle of healing. Thank you for seeing past appearances. I will always be grateful for your ability to have me try new things and never complain. I thank God every day for you.

Ty Guy, oh to have half of your spirit. What an incredible answer to prayers you are.

Finally to Sydney, who is now big enough to know that Mommy had cancer. What a beautiful girl you are, inside and out. I am so grateful for you.

About The Author

Heather Jose is a five year survivor of stage IV breast cancer. Her story is written to inspire others to fight the battles of life. The letters within the book were written throughout her journey and they were distributed to hundreds of people. Heather Jose has published works in magazines and has been asked to speak on various occasions. Heather lives in Michigan with her husband Larry and their children Sydney and Ty.